89

SO LONG, FAREWELL AND THANKS FOR THE CHURCH?

To
Charles and Beryl Stuart
They sowed the first seeds of faith and justice in my heart

SO LONG, FAREWELL AND THANKS FOR THE CHURCH?

Morris Stuart

SCRIPTURE UNION

Scripture Union, 207–209 Queensway, Bletchley, Milton Keynes, MK2 2EB, England.

Copyright © Morris Stuart 1992

First published in 1992 in Australia by Hodder & Stoughton. This edition is published by arrangement with Hodder Headline Australia Pty Limited. First published in the United Kingdom by Scripture Union, 1996.

ISBN 0 86201 992 3

British Library Cataloguing-in-Publication Data
A catalogue record for this book is available from the British Library.

Cover design by Mark Carpenter Design Consultants.
Illustration on page 33 by Brady Senior.

Phototypeset by Intype London Ltd.
Printed and bound in Great Britain by Cox & Wyman Ltd, Reading.

🍃 *Contents* 🍃

🍂 *Foreword* 🍂

I knew Morris Stuart during his years in London. He met us squarely, holding us to a personal relationship with the living Christ and, at the same time, insisting on his Lord's concern about racism and inner urban deprivation in Britain. He has kept his faith in spite of the discouragement of those who have turned away, whether from the church or from the social justice questions. The gospel for Morris Stuart has always meant the application of personal faith in Jesus to these questions.

Comfortable Christians are at home in the prevailing world order. They continue to hope that wealth and opportunity may 'trickle down' to those citizens who are shut out from choices which so many of us take for granted. Morris presses us to ask the uncomfortable questions about why thoughtful people stay away from the church or bid us 'So long, farewell and thanks'.

This book expresses a sharp tension. On the one hand are those who claim that the Holy Spirit gives them strength, protection, success as individuals, without questioning their social philosophy, often pleading that one person can do little to change the course of events. Yet many are 'gatekeepers of opportunity'. They have the power either to open the gates to jobs and opportunity, or to keep them firmly closed.

On the other hand are those who respond urgently to the promise of social justice made by God in Jesus. This involves staying with the complex issues in our world till we understand what is meant by 'engaging the structures and powers' of this world. For this we need the patience and perseverance to unravel the web of disadvantages in which so many people's lives are entangled.

Morris Stuart avoids being simplistic. He carefully acknowledges the importance of personal integrity and a relationship at this level with God, but he always points beyond this to a wider integrity. In the Decade of Evangelism, here is a challenge to the church to live as servants of the kingdom of God. Then some of those who are saying 'Farewell' may want to hear our good news.

† *David Sheppard, Liverpool*

❧ *Preface* ❧

Janice and John Bevan are in their early 40s. They have very little to do with the church nowadays. Both are disillusioned. Janice's disinterest and disenchantment are almost unshakeable. At times she can become quite bitter, quite vitriolic. John never seems to tire of attempting to make sense of what happened to them. Currently, he is trying various strands of 'tried and true' or 'avant-garde' psychology. Psychotherapy may well be their 'salvation'.

Over twenty years ago they were missionaries, committed, dynamic, self-sacrificing and exuberant. They were 'new wine' with which the 'old wineskins' could not cope. So, they left the established church and, with others, pioneered a new church within the charismatic renewal movement.

The Bevans spent their time teaching, preaching, counselling and enabling their flock to grow, to struggle and, hopefully, to be faithful to Jesus. They encountered enormous difficulties as their fellowship lurched from excitement through extremism into introspection, balance, disappointment, decline and disintegration. It was a traumatic pilgrimage, and now they are refugees!

Theirs is a story of lost hopes and dreams, of regrets of a wasted youth, of financial deprivation brought about by pursuing ideals now considered hollow. Now they have no faith, no God, no church, no money and no material props. At the present time there seems no hope of them ever returning to the fold. Or is there?

Max Broadbent used to be a radical (disciple). He abandoned the church in his native Australia in the mid-Seventies, because it failed to exercise courageous political choices at a time of great national turmoil. For conscientious reasons he objected to the Vietnam War, now discredited by Robert Macnamara, its principal architect. True, the church ought to have been more prophetic. It *did* fail to exercise courage and leadership at a time of deep national and political crisis. But Max, I think, was somewhat short-sighted when he 'jumped ship'. His righteous indignation soon turned to anger and then bitterness against the church – and God – leaving him bereft of any purpose, joy or even energy to respond to pressing social and political issues.

Like Janice and John, Max too is now without church, faith or God. Today he is left only with the symbols of his personal achievements: a PhD, social position and material comfort. He is looking forward with a great deal of ambivalence to his retirement on a fat pension. The most likely scenario for this period of his life is that of endless days exploring with others on a similar pilgrimage the wasted opportunities, the regrets and the faded hopes for a world which he had once thought he could have a part in transforming. The only light relief in prospect for Max is the punctuation of this gloom with indulgences made possible by the material rewards conferred upon him by the very society he had hoped to change.

I met Phineas Ramphele in Switzerland in 1974. He was then a Pentecostal minister in urban South Africa. His broad black smile, his zeal for God, his love for people and, above all, his passion for justice were convincing and infectious. As the heat of Apartheid further intensified, he simply disappeared. Ten years later I enquired of him. No one knew for certain, but the word was that he too had dropped out somewhere in the United States, burnt out by Apartheid's heat and frozen out by lack of support from his church. A pity, because the wider church played such a seminal role in that struggle for justice, and history has vindicated Phineas' stand. Yet in the Seventies he was alone. Was his only option, then, the African National Congress' armed struggle? Once a Christian radical, now he too has become a refugee.

I have changed their names and I have told their stories in such a way as to protect their identity, but these are the stories of real people. They are also representative of many who grew up in the socially volcanic climate of the 1960s and 1970s; they really did believe in a new world coming. They had hoped for a church which was equal to the challenge. They left because, in their view, the idea had arrived on time but the church was not ready for it. So, for them it was 'so long, farewell, and thanks for the church'.

৩ ৩ ৩

Then there is myself! But for the 'accident' of grace, the Black Panther movement would have swallowed me up in the Sixties. I was born a descendant of slaves in the British colony of Guyana in South America. My graduation to adulthood coincided with the 'wind of change' which Harold Macmillan said was blowing across Africa and consequently blowing the British and European empires away. This was the social and political cradle in which my Christian faith had its beginning and in which it was nurtured. I then lived for some years in London. This period coincided with the civil rights movement in the United States.

This time in history was turbulent as well as hopeful. There were massive famines and droughts in India, while in Africa all the constructive energies of the newly independent nations were being unleashed. In the United Kingdom, politicians and leading historians were inflaming the race relations context by making carefully crafted but socially obnoxious statements. Britain was warned of the modern spectre of 'the River Tiber foaming with blood'! Immigrants were being 'encouraged' to 'voluntarily' repatriate to their countries of origin. Black Christians were being turned away from 'white' churches, and therefore formed their own. In the United States, Martin Luther King and John F Kennedy were assassinated, and Stokeley Carmichael coined and popularised the phrase 'Black Power'.

For any young black Christian this was a perplexing situation presenting hard options. Meanwhile, in the church the most common sermon addressed the social problem of the miniskirt – major statements about minor garments! Obviously the miniskirt was of greater concern to God than poverty, hunger, war, injustice and racism to which the majority of God's human creatures were being subjected! And the environment groaned; but it must have been a very silent groan for no one heard it, until we started choking on the fumes of our affluence.

But I stayed with the church. Today I am a pastor in a community church in Melbourne, Australia. In 1965 I almost became a refugee. I had had enough of what I saw as the church's hypocrisy over the issues of race, hunger, injustice and revolution. Mine was not so much an intellectual crisis of faith. Such matters never really distressed me, though I have always pursued them with vigour. My problems with the church concerned the issue of Christian ethics – not Christian personal ethics, but Christian *social* ethics. Why did the God of the prophets of the Old Testament and of the Jesus of the New Testament seem to me to clash so harshly and so obviously with the evangelical world-view of the 1960s?

I stayed in the *church* because I concluded that the God

of the Bible was right and that *this* church of my experience was wrong. I would stay and work at my salvation. That meant working for renewal within the Christian community. I would work towards recapturing a vision of the kingdom of God as the dominant social reality and world-view for Christian disciples. I would live and work with other Christians to affirm that God calls us to follow the Jesus of the New Testament, who came to rearrange the social order: to scatter the proud and to lift up the lowly; to fill the hungry with good things and to send the rich empty away; to preach the gospel which is good news to the poor (otherwise it is a false gospel). Jesus lived his life as a servant and gave it on the cross as a ransom for many. He died on the cross for the forgiveness of our sins; but on that cross he also conclusively 'disarmed the principalities and powers', exposing them and 'triumphing over them' (Col 2:13–15). His work will be accomplished when, in the end, he returns to restore all things and all persons to their proper place and relationship within God's economy, so that the kingdoms of this world will finally acknowledge his abiding Kingship and rule.

I stayed in the church neither to enhance its complacency, nor to remain silent in the face of its silence and complicity with the status quo which oppresses the poor and discriminates against black people, brown people, red people and women. I would not stay in the church to affirm its general belief in social and political conservatism. Nor would I stay to identify with the rampant individualism, the materialism, the pomp, ceremony, opulence and affluence which characterise so much of the contemporary church, alienating it from its founder, the Nazarene carpenter, from its contemporary social context and especially from the poor and oppressed.

I have always been a thoroughly political animal. It goes with the history! First, there was my birth in a colonial village and my nurturing in a family with a father deeply involved in grass-roots politics and the Guyana Trades Union movement. Next, there was my own involvement in politics and political debate as a high school junior and my participation in the great general strike of 1963. Then there was the period in London as a political activist, tramping the streets of the city to drum up support for my preferred political party in general elections in Guyana. And then the compelling vision of the like of Amos, Micah, Isaiah and Jesus. All this and more forms the backdrop to my insistence in later years that my evangelistic ministry ought to reflect – in its choices, its geographical context and its message – the reality of the serious problems of racism and inner urban deprivation in Britain in the Seventies. This meant my deliberate decision to be involved directly in anti-racist campaigns. The gospel for me has always meant the application of personal faith in Jesus to *all* of these questions.

Following Christ is not simply a matter of tithing 'mint and dill and cummin' but especially about not neglecting 'the weightier matters of the law, justice and mercy and faith'. It *is* about matters of personal behaviour, but also, and especially, it is about righteousness, justice and the integrity of creation.

Back to Max Broadbent: I said to him recently, 'You should never have left.' When people like Max leave the church, it makes life much more difficult for those of us who stay. As the flow of refugees increases, so the number of radicals decreases, imposing a greater burden on the integrity of the gospel. The 'refugees' and the 'radicals' need each other today, and the church – the people of God – needs them both, in order to craft a new coalition of faith in Jesus the equaliser, the divine Servant, who had the power to change the world and the courage to suffer in order to achieve that change. He calls us all – refugees, radicals and the rest – to follow him. But, to follow Jesus, choices need to be made and sides need to be taken.

❧ ❧ ❧

This book is not a broadside against the church. I do not try to examine why Janice and John, Max and Phineas left, or even why I stayed. That I am not an expert on resolving the problem of disenchanted disciples and spiritual brain drain will quickly become obvious. Instead, I have tried to write a book with passion about the kind of vision that has kept me in the church and which, I think, could have kept my friends there too. If they had understood this vision, truly believed it and practised it, and were encouraged and supported in their pilgrimage and struggle by their sisters and brothers – who knows? – they might still be here with us.

This document is a tract. It is about the kingdom, the church and society. It is about discipleship that takes all of these seriously, because it is a discipleship that takes Jesus the Nazarene carpenter seriously. It is about making choices and changing sides. It is about exercising a preference for the poor as the grid through which *all* faith and discipleship are to be sifted.

There is enormous need in the world today. In the face of this, our agenda as disciples is clear: salvation, justice and preserving the integrity of the creation. But the church is also in deep need. Only a complete reformation of the life of the church can match the needs of both the church and society with the demands of biblical vision. Kingdom-centred attitudes and lifestyles that shape social structures, human relationships and ecological responsibility are essential. These will speak of the kingdom of God truly active in the world.

The church in the United Kingdom today is very different to what it was two decades ago. Sermons about the mini-skirt are no longer on the agenda! I clearly remember, during the Seventies, addressing a private meeting of evangelical leaders in London upon my return to the UK after minister-ing in Australia and New Zealand for about eighteen months. I shared that I felt as though I had returned to a tired country and to a tired church. Only one of the leaders present begged to disagree. The others concurred that, sadly, this was a fair description of the church at that time. What a difference a couple of decades have made! Despondency has given way to hope. A new confidence pervades churches of all denomi-nations. The charismatic movement, which influenced and blessed so many in the 1960s and 1970s, is now more preva-lent and has recently experienced its own renewal. The pro-liferation of new 'celebration weeks' and the increasing number of large churches – some of them in inner-city, so-called 'working-class' areas – all combine to paint a very different, more vibrant picture of life in the churches today.

In addition, if you look in the right places, all across the world today there is quite an upheaval within 'established' and 'new' branches of the historic church. The charismatic renewal 'restoration' movements, discipling movements, the community movement, Vatican II, the Catholic charismatic and renewal movement, the burgeoning contemporary rock-and-roll music industry, the plethora of new churches, the Radical Discipleship movement, the Moral Majority, the move towards the restoration of religious freedom in societies which used to be Marxist, and the enormous growth of churches in the two-thirds world – all have had the com-bined effect of conveying a sense that there is enormous and constructive ferment within the body of Christ. Together with the church growth movement, the evangelism industry agrees – God is alive on Planet Earth, especially through the current manifestations of the church. All this activity suggests growth and, as a result, it may be claimed that there is a radical restructuring of life, worship, mind and mission taking place within the church today.

But is this really the case? Clearly there are a lot of people joining the church. It may seem odd, therefore, to be writing a book that takes as its starting point the experiences of those who have left and are still leaving. Yes, there is an enormous party going on, but some very faithful and dedicated people, who revel in God's grace, are clearly feeling nauseated. Why? Is their departure the action of unspiritual and ill-tempered people, or does it represent a prophetic challenge to those of us who have remained? Their departure could be a reminder for us that noise and activity do not always indicate life. Often these things are a smoke-screen obscuring the fact that there is little of substance. The reality behind the ferment may be an illusion. (Remember the prophets of Baal on Mount Carmel, 1 Kings 18.)

Yes, there is life and ferment, but there is also froth and bubble, the sounding of gongs and clanging of cymbals. We must be wise and discerning enough to spot the difference, and prophetic and compassionate enough to nurture the new life.

ᥫ ᥫ ᥫ

Amidst the fluctuating fortunes of our history, and the religious fads that have coloured the seasons of our faith, Christians are faced with one perpetual reality: we live in a world of great need, suffering and injustice. Our radicals and refugees feel a deep sense of Holy Spirit passion about these things and long to put them right. 'Your kingdom come, your will be done on earth as it is in heaven' is their inspiration. That is the goal of discipleship. Encounter with the Christ of God initiates a life-changing relationship with God, which is then caught up in a world-changing enterprise called the kingdom of God. As long as seasons of 'renewal' and 'refreshment' in the church are not matched by fundamental and far-reaching changes in society, the flow of refugees will continue, and the constant claims of divine refreshing will increasingly have a hollow ring.

The Nineties broke fresh with promise. In Europe and Africa especially, Communism was effectively consigned to the scrap heap of history. So also in time was Apartheid. Unbelievably, the conflict in Northern Ireland showed signs of giving way to peace. And, flushed with 'success' in the Gulf War, President George Bush proclaimed a 'new world order', declaring that the time had come to end Arab-Israeli conflict. By the mid-Nineties, however, this 'spring' in world affairs proved to be short-lived. New menaces were appearing on the international scene. In the former Soviet Union and Eastern Europe a plethora of regional conflicts arose, the worst of these in Chechnya and Bosnia. The Afghanistan civil war still rumbles on interminably and apparently without solution. George Bush's 'new world order' was looking more and more like the old world of death, decay and *dis*order.

Though there is still scope for optimism that there will, eventually, be peace in Ireland, today the heart of Africa is being torn in pieces by civil war in the Sudan and Somalia. The Hutu and Tutsi in Rwanda and Burundi are engaging in one of the most tragic episodes of genocide this century. This, in a region which only a generation before had been blessed by the East African revival. While the church has been an agent of reconciliation and healing, there have also, unfortunately, been examples of church communities participating in the genocide.

How we need to ensure that divine 'refreshing' and social transformation are two sides of the *same* coin. Under no circumstances are we to relegate the issues of justice and mission to the position of being a much later, or even optional, consequence of the outpouring of the power of God on the church. Our discipleship needs to be constantly challenged by this equation: we in the fortunate West luxuriate in our affluent lifestyle, choking in the atmosphere of our abundance, while globally the poor die in millions, a silent yearly holocaust. Any true spirituality, or 'refreshing', or 'outpouring of the power of God' must impact on the pitiable and oppressive condition of the vast majority of humanity – that world which God loves and for which Christ died. God wants us to be faithful. To be indifferent to the plight of modern humanity and the environment today may be described as tragic. A simple person would call it murder and plunder. We all need to repent.

This book proposes a vision with seven strands. It is, in part, my own response to the inspiration of the Spirit as I have sought to be faithful to Jesus' prayer, 'Your kingdom come, your will be done on earth as it is in heaven'.

1 Jesus, the Saviour who takes away the sins of the world, is the equaliser and the great social rearranger. His gospel is good news to the poor and oppressed. Luke described Jesus as defining his mission simply and directly: 'The Spirit of the Lord is upon me, because he has anointed me to preach good news to the poor' (Luke 4:18).

2 God's business is building the kingdom which penetrates every nook and cranny of creation: '... all things were created through him and for him. He is before all things, and in him all things hold together' (Col 1:16,17). Christian disciples are called to co-operate in this enterprise.

3 God is not involved in anything that is not essential. The physical creation is important. It must be cared for and its integrity maintained: 'The Lord God took the man and put him in the garden of Eden to till it and keep it' (Gen 2:15).

4 The kingdom is about salvation and justice for the human creature who is the image of God and made 'a little less than God' (Ps 8).

5 The kingdom is about the divine triumph over principalities, powers and all structures that govern human existence and the creation. At the cross Jesus 'disarmed the principalities and powers and made a public example of them ...' (Col 2:15).

6 Mission is engaging in costly compassion and practising justice: 'Woe to you Pharisees! for you tithe mint and rue and every herb, and neglect justice and the love of God ...' (Luke 11:42a).

7 Mission is taking seriously the Christian community's social and political responsibility. It is exercising a preference for our partners in the kingdom – 'the wretched of the earth'.

What I have written has arisen out of the laboratory of life and ministry in a variety of contexts, especially from my experience in South America, the United Kingdom, Australia and New Zealand over a period of almost thirty years. My most recent context (fourteen years) has been within a Christian community church whose beginnings stem from the era of the counter-culture. We describe ourselves as 'a group of believers attempting to be faithful to the teachings of Jesus as they are to be lived out in twentieth-century

Australia. We believe that a personal relationship with Jesus as Lord through his Holy Spirit is vital and is the only basis for fulfilled and transformed living. God has called us to holy living and dedicated human service to our fellow Christians and to the wider society. We strive to honour Christ in our midst, to love one another warmly and sincerely, and to love and serve our fellow human beings'.

This defines the meaning of 'church' for us and is the sense in which this much maligned and misunderstood word is used in this book. Fundamentally, the 'church' is the people of God. It is neither a denomination, nor an organisation, nor a religious structure. It is not simply a human institution, nor is it a place to which people go to engage in cultic activities: singing hymns, saying prayers, listening to homilies or sermons, or conducting 'worship services'.

The church is not a place to which we go but a people to whom we belong. It is that one nation under God which transcends national boundaries, social barriers and even time; which celebrates in community its life and faith; which expresses that life and faith at different times, in different places, through particular communities of Christians and through particular structures and activities. The church is the people of God, their relationships, their ministries, their life in community and their faith in God in dynamic inter-relatedness.

In the fairly sizeable community that we are – approximately 700 men, women and children – there is a diversity of Christian experience. Not all have heard the 'vision' and not all who have heard it fully understand it. We are all at different stages of our pilgrimage. But the broad outline is there to see, to experience and to participate in. We are 'standing' in what I am writing about. Daily we seek to be more faithful to the kingdom as we understand it, and constantly we endeavour to expand the boundaries of our understanding.

A word of explanation: at the end of each chapter are questions for reflection or group discussion. These are simply pointers; you may have your own. They attempt to assist readers to move from theory to practice.

My hope is that this book may assist in some way toward stemming the constant tide of refugees from the church. It may also encourage and liberate those of us who are still there into the freedom of faithful kingdom discipleship.

Morris Stuart, Melbourne

❦ *Acknowledgements* ❦

I wish to record my sincere thanks to all the many people who have contributed to this book: my pastoral and leadership colleagues and members of our community church, Truth and Liberation Concern, in Bayswater, Melbourne; the people who have participated in our leadership training programme 'Foundations for Christian Service' – your searching questions pressed me, and your responses have encouraged me over many years!

My thanks also to the two Sues and Colleen; to Georgina whose word-processing fingers bear the imprint of many drafts and redrafts; and to Donna, my gratitude for an inspired title.

I owe a great debt to Shirley Watkins, the managing editor of Hodder and Stoughton Australia for her patience and encouragement. My thanks also to Alison Barr and Josephine Campbell of Scripture Union for all that they have done in bringing this revised manuscript to production.

And last but by no means least to Barb Stuart, my steadfast and long-suffering friend.

❦ ❦ ❦

I also wish to thank the following publishers for permission to quote from works for which they hold copyright: **Herald Press**, Scottdale: Penn (US) – *The Upside-Down Kingdom*, © Donald Kraybill (1964), *The Original Revolution*, © John Howard Yoder (1971), *Christ and the Powers*, © Hendrik Berkhof, trans. © John Howard Yoder (1962); **Kefa Sempagni** – for the extract from his article in *Eternity* magazine, December 1978; **Lion Publishing** – *Christ and Violence*, © Ronald Sider (1980); **Marshall Pickering** (an imprint of HarperCollins Publishers Limited) – *Issues Facing Christians Today*, © John Stott (1984, 1991); **Paternoster Press Limited** – *The Christian View of Science and Scripture*, © Bernard Ramm (1964); **W H Allen** and **Minerva Paperbacks** – *A Dry White Season*, © Andre Brink (1979, 1992); **Wm B Eerdmans Publishing Company**, Grand Rapids: Mich (US) – *The Politics of Jesus*, © John Henry Yoder (1972).

🌿 Chapter 1 🌿

Jesus the Equaliser

In the Western context, the Sixties were replete with symbols for the new teenage subculture: the Rolling Stones, Bob Dylan, Jimmi Hendrix and, of course, the Beatles – 'Eleanor Rigby', 'Nowhere Man' and 'Sgt Pepper' became familiar vocabulary. Girls fainted, box office records were smashed, the Apple Empire was built, and it all began with some rather inane lyrics about an unknown young woman – 'She loves you, yeah, yeah, yeah . . .' *ad nauseam*. The Beatles once commented during those heady days that they were 'more popular than Jesus'. They were right, of course, then! But it was a funny thing to say, really, when one considers that Jesus was never in the popularity stakes.

Any assessment of Jesus should concentrate not on his popularity but on his endurance. Jesus was never very popular. Well-known, yes; famous, certainly; but never popular. His contemporaries heard him gladly, yet they crucified him. He has never represented the mainstream of society's aspirations, never truly reflected its hopes and dreams, nor intruded upon its life. During the years of his Palestinian ministry it was the Roman emperors and governors, the Jewish priests and hierarchy, the Zealots and the Essenes – those first-century drop-outs – who influenced life. Jesus and his disciples were a sideshow. Yet he has outstayed them all, enduring for almost two thousand years, during which time he has become the very measure by which many other lives have been assessed. Any book that attempts an account of Christianity needs to begin with some statements about Jesus, the person of Christianity. All faith is based and modelled on him. His was the 'one solitary life' of influence unsurpassed. The uniqueness of his person, his claims, his words and actions, his death and resurrection mark him out for special attention.

No one disputes that if humanity lived by his ideas, the world would be a kinder, more just and pleasant place for all creatures to live in. But there's the rub. No one wishes to disagree with or criticise Jesus, but no one wants to obey him either. There is a cost involved. It is the radical change of mind and heart which moves us to serve not ourselves and our own interests but the good of others. What Jesus said sounded good, was praiseworthy, possibly even practical, but *very inconvenient*. So, if we don't wish to take him seriously, we have to believe that he never really meant what he said!

One thing is certain: *Jesus of Nazareth came to rearrange things*. After his brief stay on this planet, nothing would ever be the same again. Notice was given of this by his mother who sang her song of praise in anticipation of his birth and its impact:

'My soul magnifies the Lord,
and my spirit rejoices in God my Saviour . . .
He has shown strength with his arm,
he has scattered the proud in the imagination of their hearts,
he has put down the mighty from their thrones,
and exalted those of low degree;
he has filled the hungry with good things,
and the rich he has sent empty away.' (*Luke 1:46–47,51–53*)

Jesus himself gave notice of his intention to rearrange things in his inaugural public address in a synagogue in Nazareth:

'The Spirit of the Lord is upon me,
because he has anointed me to preach good news to the poor.
He has sent me to proclaim release to the captives
and recovering of sight to the blind,
to set at liberty those who are oppressed,
to proclaim the acceptable year of the Lord.' (*Luke 4:18–19*)

Other descriptions of his coming confirm him as God's *key* to putting right what is wrong in the world and creation. Jesus is described as the light which penetrates the darkness of the world of human beings, their values and lifestyles (John 1:1–4). He is described as the very embodiment of truth, the key to all that is real in the universe (John 1:17). He is described as the very image of God and the quintessence of humanity (Col 1:15). He is described as the very cause, centre and purpose of all created reality. All things were created by him, for him and remain in existence because of his activity. Jesus is creation's beginning, end and purpose, but he is also *creation's sustainer*, its *glue* (Col 1:15–19). He is also described as the hope of creation's eventual restoration (Col 1:20). Clearly here is a Jesus who cannot be contained either by history or by theology.

Certainly he is immersed in history, but he is larger than cosmic life itself. He is the Christ of history but also the

Lord of history. He is the Redeemer who will 'save his people from their sin', but he is also the *cosmic Redeemer*, the one whose salvation work is as broad as the creation itself, including all time, space, history, authority and all reality. He is a cosmic Saviour, and his work of salvation, his kingdom work, is the complete restoration of all things and people to their proper place and relationship with their Creator and with their fellow creatures.

Everything, whatever it is, wherever it is and whenever it has existed, has been created and is sustained by Jesus and encompassed within his kingdom work of restoration. Jesus' salvation work is not simply a personal event and transaction. It is not even a personal event with social and cosmic consequences. Salvation is cosmic in scope. Salvation is Jesus and his kingdom work breaking into history, breaking out everywhere in creation, and forever breaking into the lives of human beings; at all times making all things new.

The work of Jesus, the cosmic Redeemer, is no abstraction. It has concrete historical expression. His teaching and signs, his life and service, his death and resurrection are all indicative of the in-breaking work of the kingdom – from the beginning of his life to its end, from Mary's song (Luke 1:46–55) to his teaching period of forty days after his resurrection as he spoke to his followers 'of the kingdom of God' (Acts 1:3).

Now after John was arrested, Jesus came to Galilee, preaching the gospel of God, and saying, 'The time is fulfilled, and the kingdom of God is at hand; repent, and believe in the gospel.' (*Mark 1:14–15*)

From that time Jesus began to preach, saying, 'Repent, for the kingdom of heaven is at hand.' (*Matthew 4:17*)

And he went about all Galilee, teaching in their synagogues and proclaiming the gospel of the kingdom and healing every disease and every infirmity among the people. (*Matthew 4:23*)

In Jesus' mind the kingdom of God was essentially what he was about. Its concerns were central to his ministry of restoring all creatures to their proper place in relationship with each other and with the Creator. The kingdom of God was the single unifying factor, the focus of all aspects of Jesus' life, ministry and message. The kingdom involved then, and involves now, a massive rearrangement of relationships, reality, power, authority, values and expectations. The last will be first, and the greatest will be the servant of all (Mark 10:42–45); the meek, not the powerful, will inherit the earth (Matt 5:5); the hungry and the poor will be uplifted and filled with good things, while the rich and powerful will be sent away empty-handed (Luke 1:51–53). Because he came to seek and to save sinners, and not to call the righteous to repentance, it is the outcast and the marginalised, the lame, the blind and the crippled who will be invited to share in his kingdom's banquet. He taught love of neighbour and of enemy. He made treatment of the poor, the hungry, the stranger and the prisoner a measuring stick of faithfulness in discipleship: 'Truly, I say to you, as you did it to one of the least of these my brethren, you did it to me' (Matt 25:31–46).

Jesus, the cosmic Redeemer, is the great social rearranger, the one who turns the world upside down. Zealots are more at home in his presence than conservatives. Though they may lay claim to him as their private evangelical possession, the Jesus whom Christians worship is not a middle-class God, a pietist Saviour, one whose purpose it is to provide emotionally invigorating and satisfying Sunday mornings – morale-boosting sessions for hard-pressed believers as we comfortable Westerners like to think of ourselves. He is Jesus of Nazareth, liberator of the poor, leveller of the high ground, the one who fills the valleys and smoothes the rough places and thus builds a new landscape called the kingdom of God in which all of God's creatures may live in peace and harmony with justice.

Jesus' inaugural in Nazareth (Luke 4:18–19), his signs, his specific sayings and teachings, the implications of his life and work, and the huge deposit in the Old Testament relating to God's concern for society, justice and the powerless (the law and the prophets which he came to fulfil), all point to the centrality and the significance of the kingdom of God to the message of the gospel and to the work of the church in its mission. The prophetic prayer, 'Thy kingdom come, thy will be done, on earth as it is in heaven', is not meant to express an abstract ideal or a vain hope. It points to a concrete reality with immediate and intermediate evidential signs of its presence. The kingdom specifically relates to poverty and injustice, racism and materialism, politics and money, human tragedy and human sin, war and peace, principalities and powers, the 'kingdoms of this world', cultures, peoples and customs. All of this kingdom work is important. There is no reality, nor human experience, nor nook nor cranny within the universe which is beyond the scope of Jesus' kingdom work of total restoration.

Jesus was the divine servant. The kingdom was his goal, its fulfilment his consuming passion. However, the route to that end was as important as the end itself. In his agenda, the values of the kingdom were as important as their eventual result. They were to be demonstrated equally by the kingdom's strategy in every part as by its eventual outcome. In Jesus' mind the end could never justify the wrong means. He was characterised by certain qualities, and his followers are called to imitate him and to take very serious heed of his example. He was characterised by willing renunciation, identification with the human condition (incarnation), servanthood, bridge-building (mediation), reconciling, prophecy and authority.

Willing renunciation. Jesus the Son willingly emptied himself of all status and power for the goal of restoring human beings to their rightful relationship with him (Phil 2:1–13).

Incarnation. He came, stayed and fully shared the human condition. He took the form of a servant, was born as a human being, 'humbled himself and became obedient unto death, even death on a cross' (Phil 2:5–8). His identification was immediate and totally non-discriminatory. By his personal history, lifestyle and associations, he made it clear that such identification would always take as its reference point the poorest of the poor, the most marginalised of the marginalised, the scum of the earth, lepers, demoniacs, prostitutes, Samaritans, publicans, sinners and women. He was, after all, anointed to bring good news of deliverance to the poor (Luke 4:18–19). Reality would always be seen by him through the eyes of their experience. He himself was born in a cowshed, spent his early life as a refugee, grew up in an obscure corner of the Roman Empire and worked with his hands. The contrast with the contemporary church, established or otherwise, is unbelievably sharp. Socially, it is light years away from its founder.

Servanthood. He described himself as the servant (Mark 10:45). His point of contact with people was always service. He healed the sick, fed the hungry, cared for the leper, restored the sight to the blind and proclaimed the good news

22

to the poor. He himself took the position of a slave (John 13). His service to others was as valid an expression of the work of the kingdom as any other activity. It was indivisible from the cross. He came to serve and to give his life as a ransom for many (Mark 10:45). His signs, healings and acts of compassion were not simply evangelistic visual aids. They were divine responses to the evil, injustice and unrighteousness in the world.

Mediating. Jesus is the cosmic bridge-builder, mediating to humankind the will and purpose of God and reflecting to and representing within the Godhead the true plight of the human condition. He is a sympathetic high priest (Heb 4:15). He is the unique bridge, the one who fills the 'in-between space' separating God and the human creature.

Reconciling. Human society is characterised by alienation – from self, from others, from the creation, from social and political structures and from God. Jesus is God's reconciler. He taught and embodied the new commandment of love – true self-love, neighbour love, love of enemy and of God. 'You shall love the Lord your God with all your heart, and with all your soul, and with all your mind ... You shall love your neighbour as yourself' (Matt 22:37,39). Because of this, Jesus potentially transformed all human relationships. He triumphed over the powers and principalities, defeating them and releasing their oppressive hold over human minds and over human society, thereby putting an end to their alienation from human beings. He is now restoring these powers to their proper role as God's servants for the common good (Rom 13). He is also restoring power to the powerless. And, by grace and through the gospel, he is reconciling human beings to the creation, teaching us to rule over and care for the earth rather than rape and destroy it (Rom 8).

Prophecy and authority. Jesus is God's great prophet and last Word (Heb 1:1–3). He announced the word of God's kingdom, that new reality which breaks into history and into people's lives to put all things right. This word was good news to the poor, an offence to the rich and the religious rulers of his day, and a threat to all temporal and secular authorities. His prophetic word encompassed all human experience and all aspects of God's creation. It was a word which affirmed that God was still active and ruling over all of creation and society.

This is the person through whom God puts things right in the world. God breaks into history through this Jesus, the divine servant, breaking into our lives, catching us up into a community of people who have been 'broken into' and 'broken together', and who have thus become fully involved in the enterprise of putting right what is wrong in a broken and marred creation. These things characterised Jesus, the divine servant. His Christian disciples are called upon to imitate him in life and in mission: 'As the Father has sent me, even so I send you; (John 20:21). The same characteristics which marked Jesus' life and ministry ought to be demonstrated by Christian disciples in our lives and mission. Like Jesus, we are to be a humble, incarnate, serving, bridge-building, reconciling and prophetic community.

This is the way in which the Christian community must take on the secular world. Unhappily, however, in spite of some notable exceptions, members of the world-wide community of faith are captives of Western culture, Western theology and Western aspirations and values. This captivity, now almost total, is a great hindrance to the growth of any authentic sense of Christian community. Western theology, structures and values have now assumed the place of orthodoxy, defining the forms of thought and action for world-wide Christianity.

I wish to give some indicators of how, through custom and habit, this has led the world-wide community of faith to depart from the example of Jesus, the divine servant, thus rendering itself ineffective and almost irrelevant within its various contemporary contexts.

For example, too many Christians have adopted a scientific and rationalistic view of reality. When considering matters of faith, or the Bible's integrity, or truth, or even 'evidences' of the power of God, their final test of what is real or not, of what is true or not, is by the scientific method. True, the scientific method is extremely useful in processing ideas and arriving at conclusions. However, it is only one among many ways of arriving at the truth. The Christian community is far too often committed to a materialistic world-view, even though it (the community) protests a supernatural source and basis for its life. As a result, many Christians find it extremely difficult to view life as a unity. Like society in general, they break life up into competing, sometimes opposing, compartments – the economic, the political, the financial, the individual, the communal, and so on.

Western society has turned this compartmentalising process into an art form. It is a society that believes in isolation and specialisation. It isolates different parts of our life that ought always to be seen and understood together. It isolates individuals from the community. It isolates the young from the old and women from men. It isolates problems from their causes, not paying sufficient attention to the reasons why difficulties arise in a particular situation. It isolates 'life's problems' from 'life'. 'Specialists' deal with death and terminal illness in our society, just in case these intrude into an otherwise antiseptic lifestyle. This isolation and specialisation occurs right across the board. For example, Western medicine has some very interesting diagnostic techniques. It isolates the symptoms (from the patient). It isolates the organ (from the rest of the body). It isolates the pain (from its causes). It isolates the patient (from the community). It isolates the treatment of the patient (from the social context).

The story is told of the visit of a British medical delegation to China for the purpose of consulting with their Chinese counterparts on various aspects of medical practice. The Chinese doctors, upon hearing about particular Western diagnostic techniques, fell about laughing. The 'isolationist' and 'specialist' approach of the Westerners seemed quaint! Unlike their British counterparts, Chinese medical practitioners had always accepted that the human body was a complex, intricate and interconnected mechanism, a unity of psyche and soma; the human being is a precious bundle of life in a context – what John Stott has called a 'soul in a community'. An illness can never truly be understood apart from its body, its history and its social context. So-called primitive societies have always known this!

Here is a fundamental flaw, yet Western churches have themselves adopted this compartmentalising process in a wholesale fashion. In contrast, the biblical view of reality is that life is one, and that things can only be truly understood within their particular context.

An illustration from the apostle Paul may be appropriate here. In writing about the crucifixion, he once said, 'For Jews demand signs and Greeks seek wisdom, but we preach Christ crucified, a stumbling block to Jews and folly to Gentiles, but to those who are called, both Jews and Greeks, Christ the power of God and the wisdom of God' (1 Cor 1:22–24). He is posing the question, 'How can the cross be understood?' Greeks would say that it ought to make sense but it doesn't, so it is foolishness. Jews would say that the cross is a denial of the power of God, so it becomes a stumbling block. But to those who understand the cross in its context, it is both power and wisdom.

Those who are influenced by Greek philosophical thinking would seek to understand the meaning and message of the cross by breaking them down into their constituent parts. However, the conclusion of such an exercise would be that the cross simply does not make sense. On the other hand, those who try to understand the cross outside the context of grace and the call of God will find that it fails miserably as a demonstration of the power of God. Unless Jesus steps down from the cross, God is shown to be spineless. But there is a 'third way'. If the cross is understood within the context of grace and God's calling, then it is indeed seen and understood as the power and the wisdom of God.

It is necessary for the world-wide community of faith, and Western churches in particular, to revise their philosophical grid so as to see reality as a unity rather than a disparity, and to understand things and experiences in their contexts rather than in micro-isolation.

❦ ❦ ❦

Another indication of the church's captivity to the Western world-view is the tendency to marginalise God with the 'religious'. This implies that God is principally concerned with 'religious' matters. Christ is seen as the Lord and Saviour of one's 'spiritual life'. The church organises its life, training, concerns, worship, finances, resources and architecture principally with the religious in mind. Too much of its literature fails to relate faith to the whole of life. The most popular literary diet is about the pursuit of the inward and the upward journey. All of this is totally invalid if divorced from the biblical revelation of God as the Lord of all life and not simply of the religious. Consequently, the community of faith is always called to be preoccupied with the enterprise of life. God is rampant and is always embarrassing the church by breaking out of its hidebound religious confines.

Because it has marginalised God to the religious, the Western church is too comfortable with a pietistic Christianity, a private faith of comfort and security for the soul which may, or may not, have any implications for the rest of life. This has made it extremely conservative both politically and socially. As a consequence, many Christians draw the most amazing conclusions, supposedly based upon the biblical record. God, for instance, is a militarist not a pacifist, a capitalist not a Marxist. God is male and not female. God is white and not black. God is conservative and never radical. Christians are not to be involved in politics unless it is the conservative politics of the 'moral majority'!

Pietistic Christianity has made God the God of rich Westerners and not the God of the poor who, it is implied, are poor precisely because they have not chosen to take God's side!

The list of conclusions is enormous, extensive and even contradictory. For example, pietistic Christianity screams in defence of unborn children, and shrugs its shoulders at the plight of millions of the already born who languish and die each day because of starvation and malnutrition. Pietistic Christianity defends the moral rightness of a just war, while condemning revolutionary responses of oppressed people as sinful violence. Pietistic Christianity insists on the absolute sovereignty of God, and yet denies God's power to change political structures. There is no concept of a God who acts in history, but only of a conservative despot who upholds the status quo. Pietistic Christianity is a culture of Christian people who are conservative by instinct and who have created a God after their own image. It is a God who fits comfortably with middle-class assumptions, middle-class values and middle-class morals, all of the things which hold middle-class society together and which hold it away from the biblical God and the gospel.

Western churches have been imprisoned by specific secular influences within Western society. They have been seduced by the cult of individualism. Positions of power and success have entrapped them within a culture of words rather than actions. (Westerners love to discuss rather than do, except in matters military or materialistic.) Faith in God and our experience in life are to be discovered and practised within a covenant community. Yet Western churches generally operate within a context of rampant individualism, which is then exported to world-wide Christianity.

This captivity to Western culture is further evidenced by the extent to which churches in this context are deeply influenced by the modern cult of success. It is no longer faithfulness but success that is seen as the sign of divine blessing. Contemporary Christians do not take up the cross daily in their vocation of following Jesus for it will clash violently with their material symbols of affluence, ease and power. It will also clash with the gadgets, the raft of plastic cards, the expense accounts and all the other symbols that sit so comfortably with the image of the successful contemporary disciple.

�◌ �◌ �◌

Tragically, the world-wide community of faith often defines 'the church' as a human institution rather than a supernatural organism. Its life, structure, priorities, strategies for mission and evangelism, and its membership make it quite clear that, by and large, it is simply a religious reflection of its culture. Perhaps the major cause of the cultural imprisonment of the Christian community is its theological starting point. It ought to have begun at the beginning with a theology that is inspired by the original creation. Instead, its starting point in arbitrating all matters of faith and life has been the 'fall' of the human creature and consequently the redemption work of Christ. This has bequeathed to it a negative and pessimistic view of human nature and of the world, which diverts energy from both the work of fulfilling the original creation commands to till the earth and govern it, and the New Testament agenda of working with God to reconcile all human beings, structures and all created things to their proper place in relationship with God.

The gospel of Jesus Christ calls the people of God to take on the world as Christ took on flesh (John 20:21b). We have briefly explored the principal barrier to fulfilling this task, that of the church's captivity to Western culture, Western theology and Western aspirations and values. There is a way out of this that may free the people of God to fulfil their divine function. This way has been charted by Jesus, the divine servant. His Lordship has specific application to the life, behaviour and, perhaps above all, the mind-set of Christian disciples. There needs to be some adjustment to their thinking that will enable them to follow the example of their servant king.

There is a tendency among Christians to behave principally as citizens within their separate cultures rather than as missionaries, as residents rather than radicals. The call of Jesus, the divine servant, is a call to follow him as a community of servants in a place of pilgrimage, a prophetic community on mission rather than a culturally captive religious community in residence. Liberation into this kind of discipleship means adopting a new agenda of understanding the Lordship of Christ, which will include the following features:

The new agenda of understanding must echo the original Christian affirmation that *Jesus is Lord of all created reality* and is calling his church into partnership with him in his work of putting right what is wrong in the world and eventually restoring it. The Lordship of Christ, like his redeeming work, is cosmic in scope.

When I became a Christian, my country was in the throes of a struggle for political and economic independence from the United Kingdom of which it was a colony. The statement 'Jesus is Lord' meant much more than either 'accepting Jesus as my personal Saviour', 'engaging in social action' or 'forgiveness for personal sin and guilt'. The Jesus who won my allegiance presented himself as the very answer to the predicament of a young Guyanese who was caught up in a struggle that was bitter. It was a social and political struggle as well as a spiritual one. Issues of injustice and oppression, wealth and poverty, war and violence were my daily food and drink. They were not issues for discussion. My very *existence* depended on the outcome of the struggle.

For Jesus to break in there he had to be something entirely other than an imported commodity that came prepackaged with all of the other bits and pieces from Europe, the oppressor. To become a Christian in such a context was to experience Jesus and his words in a way that most Western middle-class Christians never do. The crisis that brings a lot of people in Western society to faith has very little to do with the cut and thrust of political struggle or the issues of injustice, unrighteousness, wealth and poverty. Issues of personal purpose and meaning are important. Issues of morality are important. Issues of release from personal guilt are important. But the gospel of the divine servant is not only about personal matters; it is also about the weightier matters in life.

Western Christianity has reduced faith to a personal and private transaction principally to do with religious matters, middle-class values and a particular view of public decency. Sin has been reduced to performing antisocial acts that are repugnant to middle-class people, and righteousness turned into a process of so shaping our lives that they win the approval of middle-class people. The Jesus who is Lord cannot be contained by such cultural parameters.

✽ The new agenda of understanding includes an affirmation that '*life is one*' and not a series of loosely connected or even disparate components. All life is presided over by Jesus, the Lord, the divine servant, who holds it all together. He upholds 'the universe by his word of power' (Heb 1:3). 'He is before all things, and in him all things hold together' (Col 1:17). When Jesus breaks into life, his in-breaking is never limited to the religious; instead, it fills all of life with Godly significance, whether in the person, society, principalities and powers, time and space, or history. This is true spirituality.

An understanding that life is one puts an end to the compartmentalising of life and frees the Christian community to look for God's kingdom at work in every place. No context is exempt, nor is any context so corrupt that it is excluded from the activity of the kingdom of God.

✽ Yet another item on the new agenda of understanding is the affirmation that *God is sovereign*. When considering the sovereignty of God, most Western theologians major on God as dictator, a divine despot who does as he pleases, chooses whom he likes and damns all the others. However, there is a fundamentally different way of understanding God as sovereign. It is a view that sees sovereignty as dynamic rather than static. God is big enough and sovereign enough to intervene in history and radically change all of life's circumstances, social structures and social conditions so as to bring in a new creation and a new order.

During the 1960s, while Western theologians and Christian leaders wrote papers and conducted discussions on civil rights, it was black Christians in the southern states of America who put their bodies on the streets. Armchair reformers criticised Martin Luther King and his followers in the Southern Christian Leadership Conference for praying on the streets. Regularly during demonstrations the marchers would kneel and pray. It was in this context that Martin Luther King said of his adversaries: 'We will match their ability to hate with our ability to love'. When those people knelt and prayed, it was not simply a device for non-violent action, a convenient political tool; it was a statement of faith. The black protesters actually believed that by engaging in prayer with a sovereign God in a context of alienation and tension their situation could be changed.

To say that God is sovereign is to affirm that the Creator can break into history and radically change life as well as the history, structures and social conditions that shape it. As a result, no problem is too big for God to solve. No issue – social, political or personal – is beyond the scope of God's restoration work. Christians have too often believed that God can only solve the small social problems, leaving bigger ones to heaven. This is not Christianity. It is an imposition of middle-class cultural values on the gospel itself. There is a need for the church to recover a biblical agenda for its life and mission, because only such an agenda has the power to free it from its middle-class captivity.

The most important item on the new agenda of understanding is *community*. Community means accountability – 'I am my brother's keeper'. My brother and sister include those of the community of faith, but also my enemy. I must live my life in accountability with others. For Westerners especially it means living our lives in accountability with the poor and the oppressed. All of our life's decisions must be made within the context of the questions 'What will this do to the poor?' and 'How is this issue viewed by the poor?' Living our lives in community with the poor will provide us with answers to some of the most perplexing questions with which we are faced in the West.

Community means the abandonment of Western evangelical supremacy and Western cultural imperialism. It means the abandonment of Western missionary ascendancy and the recognition that we belong to a world-wide family under God within which there are those who are far more experienced than ourselves in dealing directly with questions of the poor and poverty, of caring for the earth and peace. We ought to look to these people for guidance.

There was a time when those who were living in other parts of the world had to accept the grace of God mediated through the lives of men and women who came from Europe to live, to share and to teach this gospel of grace, even though some of these missionaries thought them uncivilised and defective! No matter. Now the relationship has turned full circle. Because of its cultural captivity Christendom has all but killed biblical Christianity in the West and has lost its way. If we open our ears and our hearts to our other family members in the two-thirds world for whom justice, righteousness and peace have been their daily food and drink, then we shall begin to find our way again. When we recognise this and willingly call for the help of these sisters and brothers, it will be a sign that Jesus the Lord is reigning again.

ed ed ed

We conclude where we began. Christianity is about a person – Jesus – and the meaning of his presence in creation. He is the cosmic Redeemer, the social rearranger, the liberator and Messiah. This is the divine servant. It was said of his earliest followers that they turned the world upside down 'acting against the decrees of Caesar, saying that there is another king, Jesus' (Acts 17:6–7). Yes, Christianity is about kings and kingdoms. It is also about acting at times against decrees and reversing the social order. It is about participating in the formation of a new kingdom whose existence is not confined to the future but ever breaks into the present.

Jesus, the divine servant, is king of a real kingdom. He is not a petty dictator, nor regional puppet, but one whose domain exceeds and transcends all other dominions. He is the Lord of time, space, history, human purpose and all reality.

The Christian community needs fundamentally to shift its mind-set. Jesus is not simply an object of mystical admiration and a focus for religious experience. He is another king. We need to understand his kingdom, its agenda and scope clearly and then place ourselves firmly and without reservation under its influence as its citizens, its missionaries and its prophets.

For Reflection/Discussion

1 Which column of the opposite chart – the left or the right – reflects more accurately your church community?

2 In the light of this chart, assess your own church community's teaching, lifestyle and ministry.

3 Make a new chart which represents your church's model and practice of discipleship.

4 Compare the charts, then list steps that can be taken to correct the discrepancy between them.

From captivity to freedom

Christian community

In captivity to Western culture, aspirations, values and theology	Freedom to be captive to Jesus, the Lord Messiah, - this captivity brings new values, aspirations, culture and a theology from the view of those at the bottom
'Greek' thought patterns	'Hebrew' thought patterns
Rationalise, specialise, compartmentalise, privatise	Life is one - things are understood in their contexts
Individualism	Community
Power and the cult of success	Servanthood and faithfulness
'Prosperity'	Responsibility and voluntary poverty
Thought patterns beginning with 'the nightmare' - the Fall	Thought patterns beginning with 'the dream' - the original good creation

❧ Chapter 2 ❧

The Kingdom – Every Nook and Cranny

Twenty-five years ago Western society was being shaken to its core. The generation that gave us the Beatles, the Rolling Stones, Germaine Greer and Timothy Leary was challenging our social and ethical norms as never before. It questioned what we believed about sexuality, drugs, women, war, peace and parents. And we got the 'permissive society', psychedelia, Woodstock, Haight Ashbury, the Apple Empire and Carnaby Street.

When John Lennon and Yoko Ono had their very public (*very* boring) Manhattan love-in, it wasn't just a crazy idea. It had a context. America was at war on three fronts. Within its urban bowels, it was at war with itself as the struggle for racial justice intensified. In South-east Asia it was fighting an unwinnable war in Vietnam. And this war was the cause of another war within, with its students, its young and its radicals – the Vietnam anti-war movement. These events had their parallels in Europe and in Australasia. In the global context, currents for change were mounting. With events like the 'wind of change' in Africa, guerrilla warfare in South America, the Maori land marches in New Zealand (to mention but a few) came a sense that something of very significant proportions was happening, that a counter-culture was emerging which would usher in far-reaching and lasting change. In California the air was alive with the promise of changing the world through 'flower power'. The 'Age of Aquarius' was on its way. The Beatles were now imploring, 'Give peace a chance', and Bob Dylan reassured us that 'The answer, my friend, is blowin' in the wind'.

The revolution did not happen. The radicals of the Sixties and Seventies have become today's (no longer so young) yuppies. The student demonstrators who brought Paris to a halt in the Spring of '68 are now technocrats, the high priests of modern French economic and administrative culture. Driving Porsches, BMWs and Volvos, and living in suburban France, they have travelled a long way from that moment in time almost thirty years ago when they had hoped to usher in another French Revolution as they forged their historic – but, alas, very short-lived – coalition with peasants and factory workers. Yesterday's radicals have become today's bourgeoisie, running corporations, lecturing in universities and jostling for political status, in the United Kingdom, in Europe, in Australasia, and in the USA where one of them now presides over the White House. Over the years realism has tempered idealism and, along the way, compassion has tempered passion. They have either 'woken up' (to the 'error' of their ways), 'grown up' or given up!

But some haven't. Occasionally one chances upon a fifty-year-old beatnik, a remnant of the counter-culture, a curious relic of a once glorious age of idealism. Like the fabled Japanese soldier found stalking the jungles of Papua New Guinea twenty-five years after the end of World War II, blissfully unaware that the conflict was over and his side had lost, these veterans solidly resist the invitation to 'come home, soldier. The war is over!'

Most others have adjusted to the status quo. Or they are dead. Or they are on their way to death. For both good and ill, they have left some indelible traces of change on the landscape of our minds and on the moral and ethical geography of our culture. In spite of this, however, there is ample evidence that today's society is, in many ways, more conservative, more materialist, more capitalist (the philosophy of 'the market' is now firmly entrenched) than it ever was in the 1960s and 1970s. In spite of the achievements of civil rights movements and anti-racist laws, today's society is more racist. Note the alarming rise of neo-Nazi movements in France, Germany, the United Kingdom, the United States of America, in various Eastern European states and in the former Soviet Union. And the present legacy of the struggle for women's rights is that we are currently, ambiguou ly, feminist and chauvinist. And uncomfortable!

Things are a lot more complex today than they were a quarter of a century ago. Society is in many ways more open but, at the same time, much less malleable, less flexible that it was then. In the Sixties and Seventies, society seemed to have less of a philosophical or ideological defence against the strength of protests and the moral righteousness of espoused causes. Its guilt was beyond reasonable doubt because its sins were self-evident: napalm scalding innocent Vietnamese children; Bull Connor's police dogs and water hoses turned on peaceful, praying blacks in Alabama; students shot down by the National Guard at Kent State University; in South Africa, defenceless Africans massacred in Sharpeville.

But things have changed. Established society today (money and power) has developed philosophies and a consistent ideology with which to defend itself against moral and ethical guilt. The rhetoric and oratory of ultra-conservatism on one hand, and the fundamentalist fervency of the thought police and their political correctness on the other, together govern our social context. Both strands have produced a pot-pourri of slogans, catch-phrases and sentiments that basically appeal to people's fears and selfishness. In addition, our current social context is a period of incredible diversity and rampant libertarianism. People no longer know what to believe or whether they ought to believe anything anyway. As a result, we are governed by a plethora of ideologies based on selfishness in a generation without absolute moral values.

∾ ∾ ∾

What ought the Christian response to be in this context? What responsibilities do we have in the light of the social and political challenges with which we are faced? What principles should govern our response? Do the circumstances of the day influence or dictate which 'issues' we should respond to and how we should respond to them? What of the community of faith, its life, spirituality and structures? What is the Holy Spirit inspiring us to do in these circumstances?

Interestingly, the church had its own mirror of the counter-culture – the Jesus movement. Thousands of young people became Christians, many converting to Jesus out of that culture. Some charismatic personalities emerged and, with vision and rhetoric, they spurred the new disciples on. There was a mushrooming of alternative Christian communities, Bible study groups and exotically named evangelistic youth movements. The slogans, the stickers, the rock music and the 'One-Way' sign became the symbols of that movement as its adherents too looked for a new world coming. There was a lot of caring: of drug addicts, of people in gangs, of people who had 'dropped out' and who had now found, in Jesus Christ, a better, truer way. These counter-culture Jesus freaks also wanted to change the church, its structure and the world. However, today very few of these communities remain. There are even fewer Bible cells, and the exotic names have all but faded into the dust of history.

In the socially sympathetic context of the Sixties, Christian radicals said many things about renewal in the church and radical change in society, which sounded prophetic. Often, though, it was the prophecy of the social echo – a shrill Christian response to issues and fashions of the day. It has to be confessed now that for the most part their bold statements were rhetoric: half-baked solutions to social problems, soft left-wing claptrap and naive prescriptions about structural change in the church and social change in society. Many of us were long on recent experience and very short on weathered wisdom! Essentially, this radicalism was really a flamboyant idealism masquerading as radical biblical vision. The evidence for this is the fruit. With very few exceptions (usually the people who did not shout the loudest), the legacy of those halcyon days has been a long trail of dismantled communities, disillusioned disciples and burnt-out radicals.

Like their counter-culture counterparts, many of the early enthusiasts and radical disciples have accommodated themselves to the status quo. Many have compromised their faith by accepting and biblically baptising the doctrine of selfishness that is prosperity teaching. Those who have resisted this trend have settled for what Charles Elliot has called 'comfortable compassion'. And the church to which they prophesied is still, by and large, a mirror of the current conservative social context. In this climate the radicals are lost, making their uncertain sound on social justice and political action, apparently unable to handle a cocksure conservatism. Yet the poor are still poor – only now there are more of them – and Christ still calls us to serve these, the wretched of the earth.

The biblical reflection, 'Where there is no vision the people perish' (Prov 29:18, AV) is very relevant here. The radicals of a quarter of a century ago had a vision but did not fully understand its implications. They were consumed by what they knew of the kingdom, but the implications were more far-reaching than they imagined. In this era of strident non-belief there needs to be a clearer vision for the people of God.

There is, amidst the darkness of the world, a lingering awareness among many people that, despite all the evidence to the contrary, human society has the capacity to demonstrate greater possibilities for good. For Christians, these greater possibilities involve an expression in society today of the lifestyle and the presence of the kingdom of God.

The kingdom of God celebrates the relationship between

God and the created order. Its purpose and values challenge all people, especially Christians, in their attitudes and actions. It encompasses eternity and time, history and human purpose, God's ultimate objectives and the church's mission, justice and peace, suffering and power, the poor and poverty, materialism and wealth, racism and reconciliation, the uniqueness of Christ not simply in relation to other faiths but especially as the central unifying reality in the Godhead's universe, as the one who is Lord and cosmic Redeemer (Col 1:15–17).

'Thy kingdom come, thy will be done, on earth as it is in heaven.' Here is the divine enterprise, the hope of Christ, the will of the Father and the work of the Spirit succinctly put in fourteen simple words. It ought to inspire universal enthusiasm and commitment among Christians. Yet, over the years of Christian history, these words have often been a theological battleground for the followers of Jesus.

ʊ ʊ ʊ

So, what is the kingdom? How does it break into history? When is it coming, or is it already here?

Christians have had a variety of answers to these questions. Some have felt that the kingdom mainly breaks into the lives of individuals, bringing spiritual benefits and reforming personal character. The values of the kingdom have only limited application to the rest of society. The principal impact of the kingdom, according to this view, is upon the life of the individual.

Others have seen aspects of the teaching and demands of the kingdom as having significance only for the life and times of Jesus and the early church. So, because they believed in the imminent return of Jesus, the early Christians could afford the luxury of a kind of ethical fanaticism towards Jesus' teaching. Of what relevance to our contemporary context is the teaching of a man whose awareness was circumscribed by the culture and geography of first-century Palestine? That ancient culture knew nothing of industrialisation, urbanisation, multinational corporations, neutron bombs or the threat of nuclear holocaust. Ideas formed, fashioned and propagated then are of no relevance today. The kingdom, according to this view, is limited to a narrow corridor of history.

Still others have located the kingdom entirely in the future. Jesus' millennial reign, inaugurated by his return, will mark the beginning of this kingdom fulfilled. The ethical demands of the kingdom and its expectations apply only to that time and have little, if any, relevance for today. The kingdom's impact and relevance are therefore postponed to an 'eternity in the future'.

These three responses, that limit the scope and relevance of the kingdom of God to the individual or to the past or to the future, distort and obscure its reality. The kingdom is not limited by geography, history, prophecy, chronology or anthropology, for the kingdom points not to the location but to the perpetual *activity of God*.

The kingdom of God is not located in territory in a geographical sense, or in history in a temporal sense, or in ideas in an abstract sense. It 'does not stand still on a particular piece of ground'.[1] It is a process being achieved, a dream being realised and a vision in the process of fulfilment.

The kingdom of God is the dynamic rule or reign of God's government, authority and power. It is God's purposeful ruling activity in creation and among and within all creatures. The kingdom of God is a dynamic and not a static reality. It therefore defies definition but not description. Jesus used pictures to describe it:

The kingdom of heaven, he said, is like a great treasure. When it is found, the finder will sell all he has in order to acquire it. It is worthy of the investment of all our resources, even our very life (Matt 13:44,45).

It is like a grain of mustard seed, the smallest of all seeds; yet when it grows, it is the largest of garden plants and becomes a tree, so that the birds of the air come and perch in its branches (Matt 13:31–32).

It is like a crop of wheat, which grows alongside weeds that an enemy has sown, awaiting the time of harvest. On that harvest day the wheat and the weeds will be gathered together, but the weeds will be burned and destroyed and the wheat will be put to purposeful use (Matt 13:24–30).

It is like light in a dark and colourless world, exposing what is evil and illuminating the signs of good that may be there (Matt 5:14–16).

It is like salt in an unsavoury and savourless society, destroying what is rotten and adding flavour to that which is bland and without meaning and purpose (Matt 5:13).

The concept of the kingdom of God is the unifying theme of the message of Jesus. It permeates his ministry and gives his gospel great coherence and clarity. But this concept is also the singular unifying theme of God's entire work in all creation, time, space and history. It comes to us in pictures, in parables, in acts, in signs and miracles, in prophecy, in judgement. The kingdom is a kaleidoscope of divine activity, constantly breaking into history, breaking out everywhere in creation and forever breaking into the lives of human beings, at all times making things new.

The kingdom breaks into life at a range of points, individual, social, historical, temporal, political and 'religious'. At all points of its in-breaking it is a spiritual, which is to say a divine, enterprise. In other words, although not every manifestation of the kingdom may be religious (which is often seen by some Christians as a synonym for 'spiritual'), all manifestations of the kingdom of God are deeply spiritual. Liberation of an enslaved nation, the judgement and destruction of a covenant-breaking nation, the destruction of evil nations and oppressive overlords, the migrations of peoples; doing justice, loving mercy and walking humbly with your God; caring for the widow, the orphan and the foreigner – all these are aspects of the dynamic rule of God at work. The work of the kingdom is as wide-ranging as history, as extensive as God's work in all creation, spanning time, eternity and the broadest possible scope of the divine purpose.

Nowhere in the Old Testament is the kingdom the same as the covenant community of faith. Nor in the New Testament is the kingdom the same as the people of God. Yet the confusion of the one with the other persists. The kingdom and the church are often identified with each other. Sometimes the words are used as synonyms for each other. Often one is made to disappear in favour of the other, so that the church becomes the kingdom and the kingdom becomes the church, at all times (consequently) obscuring the true nature of each.

Popularly, we may describe the kingdom of God as the *interface* between God and all creation. Everything God does in relation to the creation is done within the context of God's rule, sovereignty and governance. The kingdom is where the Creator meets the creation. However, the creation is extremely diverse and God's rule in each sphere is correspondingly diverse. We have to take a theological journey into this diversity for a particular purpose. Contemporary

Christianity has a tendency to contract the concerns of God to suit its comfortable convenience. We need to see the bigger picture. God is neither a figment of our evangelical imagination, nor a creature of our culture, nor a prisoner of our religious agendas.

The diversity of God's creation may be summarised in four categories: the realm of eternity, the world of persons, the realm of principalities and powers, and the realm of the material universe.

The realm of eternity. The big picture extends to and includes God's creation and rule in the realm of eternity, that habitation of God which is 'before' and 'beyond' all time, space and all other reality. In this realm the angels, messengers and ministering spirits, the cherubim, the seraphim and the entire range of heavenly beings were created and exist. God rules in this domain by will. Creatures of eternity do as God requires. They can do no other. They are created not so much to respond in obedience but to act under direction. Creatures and creation in this realm are inextricably linked to God's will and intentions. When creatures within this realm choose not to function as messengers of God's will, they cease to be creatures of eternity and become intruders in the realm of time and space.

Long 'before' time and space were created and humanity was brought into being, the dynamic rule of God was asserting itself in the realm of eternity. By eternity we do not mean the vague concept of the elongation of time whether into eternity past or into eternity future. By eternity we mean the habitation of God, a realm of reality and existence that is altogether different to the human realm of time, space and history. By exercising the divine will among creatures and creation in this realm, God has demonstrated, and continues to demonstrate, kingdom rule in the realm of eternity.

The existence of this realm of the creation and God's rule in it need to be taken seriously by Christians today. Our contemporaries are interested in the paranormal, in quantum physics, in the questions of origin and destiny, in whether there is a world of reality beyond the visible. In relation to this interest, personal speculation, guesswork, fantastic claims and fairy tales abound. Tragically, the Christian community, its preachers, teachers and writers do not always help people in their search. Because of the ridiculous and unbelievably simplistic statements that are made concerning reality beyond the realm of sense-experience, we often give the impression that we too have a preference for guesswork, fantasy and fairy tales rather than for common sense and plain statements.

The biblical record presents us with a no-nonsense, common-sense view of the reality beyond the physical. It simply claims that beyond the physical there is one reality – God – who is benevolent, personal, intelligent and imaginative, autonomous, ubiquitous, moral and accessible. This God crafted the visible from the invisible, the finite from the infinite, the temporal from the eternal. From this eternal habitation the rest of creation is seen, superintended and sustained. This explains both the 'loneliness' of the human creature and its quest for a home within creation. The biblical record further asserts that the key to finding that home and to curing that loneliness lies in human beings experiencing relationship with God whose kingdom work in the realm of eternity ever presses in on all human experience and earthly reality. Human beings will find this to be so whether they accept those claims and put them to the test in their social and personal experience, or whether they reject them and take excursions into fantasy and fairy tales.

The world of persons. Here God upholds the universe and all creatures, working as creator, preserver, sustainer and judge of all life. For 'all things were created through him and for him. He is before all things, and in him all things hold together'. God's kingdom works in this context to hold the creation together. All God's human creatures, just or unjust, benefit from this superintending of life, of the seasons, the sun, the moon, the rain, and all else. Everything benefits from God's continuing dynamic activity in the creation.

God's kingdom is also at work in the world of persons where this world affirms the image of God in the human creature. At creation, the human creature was made in God's *image*: 'in the image of God he created them; male and female he created them'. At creation, the human creature was given a *mandate* – a commission to multiply and fill the earth, to tame and work it, and to rule for God over it (Gen 1:26–28). At creation, the human creature was provided with an appropriate *context* within which that image might be expressed and the mandate exercised: 'You may freely eat of every tree of the garden; but of the tree of the knowledge of good and evil you shall not eat, for in the day that you eat of it you shall die' (Gen 2:16–17). The image, the mandate and the context belonged together. Under the rule of and in fellowship with God, there was harmony and peace between all aspects and creatures within the creation. However, the human creature shattered this harmony with a wilful act of disobedience that broke fellowship with God. Consequently, there is now a long-lasting, deep and damaging effect on all creation. We have come to describe this tragic situation as humanity's 'fall'.

The Fall radically altered the *context*: 'therefore the Lord God sent him forth from the garden of Eden, to till the ground from which he was taken. He drove out the man . . .' (Gen 3:23,24). The Fall had a detrimental effect on the *mandate*. Procreation and work were originally given as blessings and as a means of affirming the image within the human creature. As a result of the Fall these activities were drastically revised. From that time, they have been carried out under circumstances of hardship and struggle: '. . . in pain you shall bring forth children . . . cursed is the ground because of you; in toil you shall eat of it all the days of your life; thorns and thistles it shall bring forth to you . . . In the sweat of your face you shall eat bread . . .' (Gen 3:16–19). These events consequently marred the *image*. Through disobedience, the human creature now had knowledge and personal experience of evil without the capacity to overcome it. This disobedience deeply distorted the perception of the image of God – of the male and female as equals.

To the image are now added the dimensions of counterfeit and contradiction. Counterfeit, because the human creature after the Fall no longer appears simply 'after the image and likeness of God'; now, with the advent of sin, the human creature strives to be as a god. Contradiction, because that which originally appeared as an image, a reflection of the Godhead in whom there is equality, diversity and unity, now appears as a hierarchy. This is indeed the marring of the image: the human creature now contradicts the nature of its Creator and distorts his image.

Yet the image of God was not removed, nor was the mandate revoked. The human creature still expresses the image of God (Gen 5:1,2). We still yearn to find God. We still live, move and have our being in God. The human creature is inextricably linked to God's image within. Through this 'image linkage' God's governance continues to be exercised, though considerably altered because of the

Fall. The work of the kingdom in the world of persons is therefore to constantly nurture and affirm this abiding image.

God is also at work in the world of persons doing the salvation work of the kingdom. Here God's purpose is the reconciliation of the creature to God and the restoration of the image of God:

For in him all the fullness of God was pleased to dwell, and through him to reconcile to himself all things, whether on earth or in heaven, making peace by the blood of his cross.

And you, who once were estranged and hostile in mind, doing evil deeds, he has now reconciled in his body of flesh by his death, in order to present you holy and blameless and irreproachable before him . . . (*Colossians 1:19–22*)

The contemporary Christian community has tended to concentrate on the redeeming and reconciling aspects of God's kingdom work as if these were its totality. However, just as God's creation and rule are diverse, so also is the work of the kingdom in the world of persons, encompassing, preserving, affirming and reconciling. Or, to put it another way, God's work in the world of person involves and includes ecology, justice and salvation. A biblically faithful world-view would affirm that God works in the world of persons by preserving, affirming and redeeming the human creature. Any reduction or abbreviation of the whole, or any prioritising of any part of this threefold work, is a cultural imposition on the gospel of the kingdom and therefore has to be rejected as not reflective of the biblical record.

The realm of principalities and powers. God exercises kingdom rule in the realm of 'principalities and powers', those structures that govern human existence: thrones, dominion, principalities and authorities, things visible, things invisible and a host of other realities that influence and control human life. In this realm God rules by ordering.

The 'powers' were originally created to be links between God and the creation in the realm of time and space. However, we do not experience them now as God originally intended. They have taken on a position of dominance and power, and would like to be worshipped as gods. The purpose of the kingdom within this realm is to disarm these powers, to expose them and to triumph over them (Col 2:15). God's kingdom work is to set the powers and principalities in their rightful place, serving the creation in general and the common good of the human creature in particular.

Far too often Western society in general and Christians in particular have assumed that an organisation or a social structure is the sum of its human parts. This is a fallacy because evidence abounds of the presence and power of corporate and spiritual forces that are much greater than the human factor. The Nazi tyranny, the anti-Armenian pogroms, the Crusades, the culture of slavery and racism, Idi Amin's reign of terror, the Gulag Archipelago, all testify to the reality of the 'powers in the air'. How many kind and gentle husbands and fathers, sensitive and caring mothers, fine and upright young women and men have been driven by the power of a tyranny to perform the most despicable acts of barbarity and cruelty against fellow human beings, on the streets of Sharpeville and Soweto, in German concentration camps and gas chambers, in Siberian slave camps, on American cotton plantations?

Human alienation and sin are legitimate targets for the work of the kingdom, but so also are the rampant oppression, the deception and the control that the principalities and powers exercise over human society and the creation.

The realm of the material universe. God's kingdom operates in the realm of the material universe, the cosmos, the world of creation, of time and space. Here the purpose of the kingdom's work is the restoration of the cosmos.

It was the original intention that the human creature would be the interface between God and the earthly creation. However, the human creature's disobedience brought a curse upon creation (Gen 3:17; Rom 8:20). God's purpose now is to reconcile all things – on earth – to himself, making peace by the blood of the cross (Col 1:20), and to restore all creation to its freedom and wholeness.

For the creation waits with eager longing for the revealing of the children of God; for the creation was subjected to futility, not of its own will but by the will of the one who subjected it, in hope that the creation itself will be set free from its bondage to decay and will obtain the freedom of the glory of the children of God. We know that the whole creation has been groaning in labour pains until now; and not only the creation, but we ourselves, who have the first fruits of the Spirit, groan inwardly while we wait for adoption, the redemption of our bodies. (*Romans 8:19–23, NRSV*)

This is an amazing reality in that it spells out the kingdom work of the restoration of the cosmos, strongly linking it to God's salvation work in the world of persons. The kingdom then is active in the church and also in the physical creation.

℮ ℮ ℮

In conclusion then, God's rule, though unified in purpose, is diverse in its application depending upon the realm of creation in which it is being exercised. This brief categorisation shows the diversity of God's creation and the diversity of God's rule. It shows that the kingdom is broader and larger than the community of the people of God, and is to be distinguished from it.

The work of the kingdom of God is truly cosmic in scope. Everything – whatever it is, wherever it and whenever it has been created – is encompassed within God's kingdom activity. The world of nature, the physical creation, human beings and their relationships, and humankind's relationship to things are all encompassed in this work. So also are time, space, history and all reality: '. . . for in him all things were created, in heaven and on earth, visible and invisible, whether thrones or dominions or principalities or authorities – all things were created through him and for him' (Col 1:16).

℮ ℮ ℮

The implications of the biblical description of the nature and character of God as creator, preserver, redeemer and judge of the world confirm God's total concern for the entire created universe. Such a biblical vision commits the Christian community to a view of the kingdom that embraces all things and all realms of God's creation. It commits the Christian community to a fundamental and far-reaching concern for contemporary society. The Christian message must address itself to the predicament of humanity and the cosmos. It must speak to the issues and needs that face us, and it must flesh itself out in every arena of life, social, economic and political. The challenge which faced us a generation ago is still current. The D Generation, who 'tuned in', 'turned on' and 'dropped out', has produced Generation X. The quest of this generation is not freedom; they know that the 'Age of Aquarius' is an illusion. While they are competent in the 'outer' world of the super-information highway, virtual reality and cyber space, their inner world is dominated by anxiety, insecurity, doubts about identity and rootlessness. As they face the end of the second millennium, they know that long after their parents are dead they will have to struggle with the great problems of ecological uncertainty, burgeoning populations and world poverty on a massive scale. Apart from their human achievements, will there be any belief system, any faith to guide, any compass to chart the way?

If the church's response to this is to retreat into private faith, personal refreshing and a culture of blessing-seekers, Generation X will produce even more refugees from the church than the D Generation did. It is only as we understand and rigorously live out the message and dictates of the kingdom of God, as Jesus the Messiah did, that we shall capture our contemporaries. Here is the Person who is the creator, sustainer and focus of all created things and persons. He answers the questions, deals with the anxieties, ends the contradictions and calls us to follow him into a kingdom where things make sense and people love each other; where people live in community knowing the security of God and work for justice for their fellow human beings.

Responsible ecology towards the physical creation, salvation and justice for the human creature, and just and caring government and social structures are all concerns of God. They are the very work of God's kingdom and ought to be the central business of the Christian community.

፠ *For Reflection/Discussion*

1 'The reason for so much poverty in the Third World is because the Missionary Movement failed to teach them prosperity.' How would you respond to this statement by one of today's internationally well-known evangelists?

2 Major biblical doctrines indicate God's concern for all life. How do you as a member of a post-modern culture fulfil the creation mandate to subdue the creation, have dominion over it and keep it (Gen 1:28)? How do you make each task and social transaction sacred?

3 In twenty-five years Indonesia has reduced the percentage of its population living in absolute poverty from 65% to 15%. What concrete steps can Generation D and Generation X take to eradicate global poverty in this age?

፠ *Notes*

1 Donald Kraybill, *The Upside-Down Kingdom*, Scottdale, Penn (US): Herald Press, © 1964, p25.

Chapter 3

Principalities, Powers and Governing Structures

I say to you today, even though we face the difficulties of today and tomorrow, I still have a dream. It is a dream that is deeply rooted in the American dream. I have a dream that one day this nation will rise up, live out the true meaning of its creed: 'We hold these truths to be self-evident, that all men are created equal'.

I have a dream that one day in the red hills of Georgia the sons of former slaves and the sons of former slave owners will be able to sit down together at the table of brotherhood. I have a dream that one day even the State of Mississippi, a state sweltering in the heat of oppression, will be transformed into an oasis of freedom and justice.

I have a dream that my four little children one day will live in a nation where they will not be judged by the colour of their skin, but by the content of their character . . . This will be the day when all of God's children will be able to sing with new meaning, 'Let freedom ring.' So let freedom ring . . .

When we allow freedom to ring from every town and every hamlet, from every state and every city, we will be able to speed up that day when all God's children, black men and white men, Jews and Gentiles, Protestants and Catholics, will be able to join hands and sing in the words of the old Negro spiritual, 'Free at last! Free at last! Great God Almighty, we are free at last!'[1]

Martin Luther King's celebrated statement on the aspirations of an oppressed people for their freedom is both eloquent and enduring. It draws its inspiration from roots that are deep in God, and asserts that freedom comes from 'Great God Almighty'! This statement is inspiring; it is also instructive, recognising that, alongside the need for people to change, there is also a need for structures to be moved and transformed.

The kingdom enterprise is concerned not only with human beings, flesh and blood, but especially with principalities and powers: thrones, dominions, philosophies and human traditions. Some Christians have too often circumscribed the agenda of the kingdom by a particular view of salvation which concentrates on 'saving the soul'. Salvation is security in the life to come, pie in the sky when you die! This is understandable historically, when life was not only fragile but relatively brief. Today, however, with the benefits of modern science, advances in technology and human achievement, life has been prolonged. Now the issues are anxiety, guilt, fear, meaninglessness and a sense of loss. And the gospel has been co-opted to respond, offering personal 'peace', tranquillity, purpose and self-acceptance.

While these agendas are important they are not the only concerns of the gospel of the kingdom.

For Jesus in his time, and for increasing numbers of us in our time, the basic problem is seen less and less in individualistic terms. The priority agenda for Jesus and for many of us is not mortality or anxiety but unrighteousness and injustice . . . the need is not for consolation and acceptance but for a new order . . . (*John Howard Yoder*)[2]

Unrighteousness and injustice represent a broader focus for understanding the nature of the kingdom's salvation, which is to do with people as well as with powers. Yes, human beings need to be reconciled to the Creator and their image restored. But the structures and systems that influence their lives and the governments that rule them need to be caring and just (Rom 13:1–5).

There is a widespread idea among Christians that the way to transform society is first to transform people. These 'born again' people will then naturally transform society! The idea sounds reasonable; however, the reality is quite different. True, at particular times in history some Christians have swum against the tide in order to redress and eradicate some social evils, for example the anti-slavery movement, the suffragettes, the labour reform movement (particularly in its efforts against child labour in Britain at the time of the Industrial Revolution), the American civil rights movement, and the struggle against the Apartheid tyranny in the old South Africa. However, it is equally clear that Christians – especially in so-called Christian countries – far from solving society's problems have often been the people who actually created them.

For example, the Philippines has long been regarded as the only Christian country in Asia, yet it has also been described as the most corrupt – a rich country with a lot of poor people. Speaking from his experience in the United States, Tom Skinner, the black American evangelist once described the church as being 'twenty years out of date and on the wrong side of every social issue'. In South Africa a so-called Christian government and society created and stubbornly maintained the greatest contemporary tyranny in Apartheid, which, they claimed, was based on the scriptures of the Old Testament. In India a secular government is doing all in its power to break down racial and ethnic divisions based on the caste system; meanwhile, American church growth theorists and strategists are, in the 1990s, still encouraging Christians to establish racially segregated churches on the basis of that very dubious theory – the homogeneous unit 'principle'![3]

The presumption that there will be an automatic flow-on from individual conversion to social transformation is simplistic and dangerous. It is simplistic because it does not work, and because it ignores the lessons of history and the pervasive power, complexity and reality of social structures. It is dangerous because that which is not the truth is always dangerous. Further, it is a presumption that lulls the Christian community into a position of compliant complacency in relation to structures that may be profoundly corrupt and corrupting.

Clearly, as we have already said, a government, a social structure or a society is more, much more, than the sum of its individual parts. There are social realities that are 'larger' than human life and that influence and even control it, individually, corporately, spiritually and politically. These realities range widely, and include social structures, ethical values, governments and their power, public opinion, religion, patriotism, human traditions, philosophies and world-views.

Human history abounds with examples of individuals and groups who have felt themselves propelled into particular courses of action by forces beyond their control. Many of the repressive measures and acts of tyranny that were carried out under the totalitarian governments of Eastern Europe and the USSR, and the atrocities of the Nazi regime, were put into effect by people who were simply 'obeying orders'. People have killed, maimed and tortured others in the name of 'king and country', only to recant and repent of their actions with the passage of the years and the benefit of hindsight.

We do not in any way wish either to minimise the power of choice that is the human creature's, or to absolve individuals of their moral responsibility. However, there is ample evidence that structures have a 'life' of their own that is both independent of, and greater than, their human constituents. Our purpose in this chapter is to explore the nature of this life and to demonstrate that it is taken seriously by the kingdom enterprise. It therefore must be taken seriously by the Christian community.

ed ed ed

Our struggle is not (simply) against flesh and blood, but (especially) against principalities and powers (Eph 6:12). What are they? Well, certainly not spooks or ghosts or things that go bump in the night! And they are certainly not vague and mysterious entities.

The biblical record presents us with a straightforward, no-nonsense view of principalities and powers; we are given examples and descriptions. The 'powers' are identified, their purpose defined, the limits of their jurisdiction circumscribed, and their activity and status clearly laid out. Human tradition, public opinion, the state of society, politics, philosophy, religion, morality, cultural and traditional values, life and death, the demands of the present and the fear of the future – these are all examples of principalities and powers.

The Bible identifies an enormous number and range of the realities that are to be regarded as principalities and powers. The following list is neither complete nor exhaustive but is certainly representative. The arrangement in the seven categories is not definitive, but it indicates something of the breadth and range of these powers.

The powers are political realities. The rulers of this age, the 'governing authorities', 'the world rulers of this present darkness', 'powers', 'thrones', 'dominions', 'principalities', 'authorities', Roman law (see Rom 13:1–5; Eph 6:12; Col 1:16).

The powers are religion and religious realities. The Jewish law, the scribes (the defenders of the law), the Pharisees (the guardians of the law), the priests (the guardians of the place of worship, the temple), rules and regulations ('do not handle, do not taste, do not touch') (see Gal 3:17–26; Col 2:20–23).

The powers are cosmic realities. The seasons (seed-time and harvest), the heavenly bodies (the sun, the moon and the stars), natural disasters (pestilence, drought, plague, earthquake, flood, wind and fire), time (things past, things present and things to come), space (height and depth) (see Gen 1:14–18; 2 Chr 7:12–14; Rom 8:38–39).

51

The powers include human misfortune. Tribulation, distress, persecution, famine, nakedness, peril, the demands of the present life and fear of the future (see Rom 8:35).

The powers are supernatural (non-material) realities. Angels, 'things invisible', the 'elemental spirits of the universe', the devil and his angels, demons (see Rom 8:38–39; Col 1:16; 2:8).

The powers are ideas ('-isms' and '-ologies'). 'Philosophy and empty deceit', 'human tradition', the wisdom of this age, human precepts and doctrines (see Mark 7:7; Matt 16:12; Col 2:8).

The powers are 'anything else in all creation'. 'Things visible', the world, the flesh, the common people (who at first heard him gladly and then became the mob who demanded his blood shouting, 'Crucify him!') (see Rom 8:39).

Individually and together, these powers have an influence as broad and as deep as life itself. They are certainly not restricted to the 'supernatural', and they are not limited to political and social structures. The important thing to understand about the powers is not whether they are supernatural or temporal, but that they all share one fundamental quality – the powers condition earthly life. They govern human existence. They were originally created by God as benevolent linkages between the Creator and the human creature, as bonds to hold life together, preserving it in God's love.

We have referred to the Fall, that disturbance which fundamentally and severely damaged the relationship between the Creator and the human creature. The biblical record also teaches that a similar disturbance took place in the harmonious relationship between the powers and their Creator. This disturbance fundamentally affected the very nature of the powers and the way in which they operate. The result is that we do not now experience the powers in the role for which they were originally intended.

Because of this dual disturbance, our human context is one of persons and powers in rebellion against God. Or, to put it another way, the kingdom enterprise is confronted with personal sin and structural sin. The *redemption* work of the kingdom enterprise seeks to end the rebellion of persons. The *restoration* work of the kingdom enterprise seeks to end the rebellion of the powers. Redemption and restoration are two sides of the one coin – salvation – which is the heart of the work of the kingdom. The two sides of this coin are eloquently expressed in the letter to the Colossians:

And you, who were dead in trespasses and the uncircumcision of your flesh, God made alive together with him, having forgiven us all our trespasses, having cancelled the bond which stood against us with its legal demands; this he set aside, nailing it to the cross. (*Colossians 2:13–14*)

This is redemption, ie putting *people* back in their proper relationship and status with God.

He disarmed the principalities and powers and made a public example of them, triumphing over them in him. (*Colossians 2:15*)

This is restoration, ie putting *things* back in their proper place and status with God.

The Christian community has always taken seriously the need for persons to be redeemed, however that is understood. But it has been less convinced that there are structures in the world which need to be disarmed, exposed and triumphed over. In contrast, the biblical record makes it quite clear that there are evil people and evil structures in the world. Both have to be tackled with the weapons of the kingdom.

ભ ભ ભ

Structures are in rebellion against God, and there are a number of ways in which the powers demonstrate this rebellion.

First, by their very nature, the powers have a tendency, ability and intention to separate the human creature from the love and life of its Creator. It is only in relationship with Jesus, the divine servant, and enabled by the Helper, the divine Spirit, that we can be assured of victory over the powers. For it is in the very nature of tribulation, distress, famine, nakedness, peril, persecution, the sword, death, life, angels, things present, past or to come, height, depth and 'anything else in all creation' to separate us from God's love and life.

Second, this tendency to separate is motivated by an intention on the part of the powers to usurp divine authority. The powers will always demand our total allegiance and our undivided loyalty in return for their 'protection' and 'benevolence'. Just as human beings do not at all times and in all circumstances exhibit their rebellion against God, so it is with the powers: they do not in every instance exhibit their rebellion. They still fulfil part of their divinely ordained function. They hold human life and society together, but in so doing, they exact a very high price: they hold people away from God.

Religion, human tradition, public opinion, accepted morality, patriotism, the state, the 'good of the nation', Western civilisation and the 'Australian (or American or British) way of life', all hold human life and human society together, preserving it from chaos. But is it not also clear that it is in the very nature of these things to assume control over human life as well? As such, these powers become gods, lords and the 'rulers of this age'. God will have the powers only as instruments, not as usurpers. Their deceptive hold over human life must therefore be broken.

Third, making effective use of their ability to deceive, the powers often instigate and sustain unlikely and unholy alliances against God. They turn 'enemies' into 'friends', united against their common enemy – the Lord of Glory. This power of deception was exposed by the crucifixion. The powers, those first-century structures that governed Palestinian existence – the Roman Empire, the Jewish religious hierarchy and the mob, hitherto sworn enemies of each other – joined forces in a formidable alliance against Jesus the Prince of Glory. The vested interests of the Roman Empire were always at odds with those of the Jewish religious hierarchy, and neither took much account of the welfare of the common people. These parties had nothing in common except that now the presence of Jesus Christ exposed their false power. This was enough! It spurred them into action together to crucify the Lord, because he threatened their power over those things that hold human society together: civil law and order, religion and popular opinion.

One would have thought that if these powers had been fulfilling their true function of acting as God's instruments, they would each have recognised in Jesus the very embodiment of their hopes and intentions. However, power and control were their hidden agenda. Their assumption of divine authority and absolute power over truth and worship blinded them to the fact they were acting against the very Lord of Glory.

The powers are hostile to God in their interests, agendas and ultimate intentions. Through a combination of separating, usurping and deceiving, they demonstrate their rebellion against God, put into effect their bondage over human minds and, consequently, enforce their enslavement of human society.

How can principalities and powers that are so at odds with the interests of the kingdom be dealt with? We may choose to avoid them. They can be overthrown; they can be accommodated; they can be 'infiltrated'. Either ignore them, or get rid of them, or seek a compromise with their power, or seek to influence them for change from within. Christians have flirted with all of these responses and with some more than with others.

Avoidance. The Pharisees and the Essenes of the first century have their descendants among the 'ascetics', the 'monastics', and the drop-outs of today. Freedom from the powers is to be achieved by separation at best, or escape at worst.

Realism. The Sadducees and the tax collectors had their descendants in the Holy Roman Empire, that political and religious hybrid which co-operated in the rampant oppression and exploitation of the peoples of medieval Europe. They also have their descendants today among those in the Christian community who remain silent in the face of the powers' oppression. Motivated by naked self-interest, they 'play the system' while, at the same time, separating their religious life from their involvement with the system and its social and political realities. Their motto is 'Save what you can by doing what is possible'. These people fail to realise that, because the interests of the principalities and powers are so opposed to the kingdom enterprise, any possibility of a new order is effectively ruled out. For Jesus, there could be no compromise. His response was blunt: 'My kingdom is not of this world'.

Infiltration. This response to the powers implies either that the powers are basically good, and simply need to be tended and nurtured by good men and women; or that they are so powerful, all we can hope to achieve is gradual reform from within. This option has appealed most to contemporary Christianity. Yet it was never a temptation to Jesus. He never seriously entertained the thought of joining either the religious or the political establishment.

'Infiltrators' believe that by being benevolent and enlightened participants from within, they can change the system. But, over time, the system manipulates, coerces, moulds and shapes the infiltrator. Dealing in compromise, it will eventually extract a price for his participation. The system will change *him*. Jesus sent his disciples out as lambs amongst wolves (Luke 10:3). But the system is very adept at turning lambs into wolves, or at least changing their clothing! Thus infiltrators risk becoming 'lambs in wolves' clothing' as the system forces them to celebrate at two banqueting tables – the table of the kingdom, and the table of the principalities.

The infiltrator cannot change the system – the powers – by being a critic from within. If we are sheep and we dress as wolves, our message will have an unintelligible sound. Then, when the crunch comes, the infiltrator will stop bleating (as a sheep would) and start baying (as a wolf does)! This is often the end of the house prophet, the 'critic from within the establishment'.

Overthrowing the system. Those who are closest to Jesus' spirit of transformation find their most appealing temptation to be the same as one of his – the urge to get rid of the powers, to destroy them utterly. This was the response that the Zealots, those first-century Jewish freedom fighters, adopted. The Zealots preferred a collision course with the powers. Armed revolt, civil disobedience and opposition to Roman taxes and tribute was their strategy. Their 'manifesto' called for the abolition of debts, the redistribution of land and the freeing of slaves, all reflective of the Old Testament jubilee legislation. It is therefore not surprising that Jesus was mistaken for a Zealot from the day he announced his intention in his inaugural to preach good news to the poor, recovery of sight to the blind, to set the oppressed free and to announce the year of jubilee. This option was an ever-present temptation for Jesus, yet it is the one that appeals least to contemporary Christianity. And contemporary Christians are hardly ever mistaken for Zealots!

It is not our purpose here to discuss the merits or otherwise of this option of overthrowing the powers, except to observe that when dealing with the powers it is the option that most appeals to the poor of the world, whether they are Christians or not. Yet this is the option that least appeals to Western Christians, who almost universally reject such revolutionary responses of oppressed peoples as evil, but who almost universally embrace the belief in a 'just war'.

Without in any way establishing an 'ethic' that supports revolutionary violence (can there be one? I doubt it!), it is nevertheless necessary for Christians to understand the circumstances under which it arises. First, the biblical record recognises that life can become intolerable, especially for the poor: 'Give strong drink to him who is perishing, and wine to those in bitter distress; let them drink and forget their poverty, and remember their misery no more' (Prov 31:6–7). Second, because of the fallen creation in which people, powers and institutions are alienated from God, many are living under pressures and conditions that their Creator never intended them to endure.

There is a delicate balance that preserves human life. On the one hand, there is the God-given instinct of self-preservation, and, on the other, the gift of human dignity. Both dignity and self-preservation are basic to human nature as being made 'in the image of God'. Self-preservation is a strong defender of the life of that image. However, sometimes dignity is so assaulted that self-preservation becomes secondary. It is at this point that revolutionary violence occurs, when the image of God says, 'Enough is enough! If I cannot live with dignity as a human, I will not live at all, and I will deprive of life those who deny me my dignity.' Christians need to recognise and to understand the basic God-given instincts that operate in these circumstances, just as they so readily recognise their own misdirection and potential for self-destruction.

❧ ❧ ❧

Jesus' life was one of constant encounter with the principalities and powers. They exercised an influence over his life in much the same manner as they do over ours. The Christian community accepts this but generally confines its acceptance to the narrow context reserved for demons and demonic activity. In common Christian vocabulary, and in popular Christian understanding, 'principalities and powers' are reduced to evil spirits, demons and the like, and these are the targets for spiritual warfare.

We have seen from the biblical record, however, that the powers cover an enormous range which includes social and political realities. Jesus' way of dealing with these realities was neither to beat them nor to join them, but to propose and to establish an alternative to them: 'The time is fulfilled, and the kingdom of God is at hand; repent, and believe in the gospel' (Mark 1:14). The kingdom of God would take shape in, among other things, a community of faith that would be the extension of Jesus' personality. Through this community, the existing structures, values and belief-systems would be confronted and challenged.

New teachings are no threat, as long as the teacher stands alone; a movement, extending his personality in both time and space, presenting an alternative to the structures that were there before, challenges the system as no mere words ever could. (*Yoder*)[4]

The system cannot be challenged or responded to by avoidance, or by realism, or by infiltration, or by violent overthrow; Jesus rejected all of these. There is a more creative way. It is the way of a new King, a new kingdom and his kingdom community. Jesus was constantly tempted to assume power to achieve his ends, but he consistently chose not to do so. To choose power would have meant accepting the 'crown' with all its compromises. Instead, he chose the cross.

The cross was not simply the event that ended his human life. It was more than a substitutionary sacrifice for the lives of others. The cross was the climax and the consequence of a life lived for the sake of the kingdom enterprise. It was the inevitable end of his provocation, confrontation and threat to the contemporary powers. His teaching about the kingdom of God, his embodiment of it and his establishment of the kingdom community guaranteed that Jesus would always be on a collision course with principalities and powers of all descriptions. Jesus deliberately chose the cross because it was the only option that was consistent with his life of caring servanthood and with the message of the kingdom that was bringing in a new order of things. He would defeat the powers not by coercive power but by redemptive suffering.

Here at the cross is the man who loves his enemies, the man whose righteousness is greater than that of the Pharisees, who being rich became poor, who gives his robe to those who took his cloak, who prays for those who despitefully use him. The cross is not a detour or a hurdle on the way to the kingdom, nor is it even the way to the kingdom; it is the kingdom come. (*Yoder*)[5]

It is through the cross of Jesus, the divine servant, that the redemption of humanity and the restoration of the universe is achieved. So also is the disarming of the powers. The cross has the power to liberate people and society from the enslavement of the powers. Hendrik Berkhof, in his excellent book *Christ and the Powers*, puts the matter eloquently:

By the cross (which must always, here as elsewhere, be seen as a unit with the resurrection) Christ abolished the slavery which, as a result of sin, lay over our existence as a menace and an accusation. On the cross he disarmed the powers, 'made a public example of them and thereby triumphed over them.' ... It is precisely in the crucifixion that the true nature of the powers has come to light. Previously they were accepted as the most basic and ultimate realities, as the gods of the world. Never had it been perceived, nor could it have been perceived, that this belief was founded on deception. Now that the true God appears on earth in Christ, it becomes apparent that the powers are inimical to him, acting not as his instruments but as his adversaries. The Scribes, representatives of the Jewish law, far from receiving gratefully him who came in the name of the God of the law, crucified him in the name of the law. The Priests, servants of his temple, crucified him in the name of the temple. The Pharisees, personifying piety, crucified him in the name of piety. Pilate, representing Roman justice and law, shows what these are worth when called upon to do justice to the Truth Himself. Obviously, 'none of the rulers of this age', who let themselves be worshipped as divinities, understood God's wisdom 'for had they known, they would not have crucified the Lord of Glory' (1 Cor 2:8). Now they are unmasked as false gods by their encounter with very God: they are made a public spectacle.[6]

It is only the 'weakness' of the cross which could have exposed the powers for what they really were. Infiltration never exposes the true nature of the powers. Accommodation with them is an admission of total defeat. Avoidance is for ostriches. Violently overthrowing the powers is a guarantee against their eventual restoration to their proper place as servants of God for the common good. It is only through the redemptive suffering of the cross that victory over the powers can be achieved. It is only at the cross that this victory is fully realised as the powers are exposed, as their weapon of control is struck from their hands, as they are triumphed over and put back in their proper place as servants and not usurpers.

It is at the cross that we have been set free from the powers, and now the whole of creation awaits eventual liberation. Since the cross, no powers can separate us from God's love in Christ, or usurp divine authority, or rule over us and the rest of creation with the power of deception. Jesus Christ is the Lord and protector, and everything in all creation will eventually acknowledge his sovereignty as each experiences his liberation.

So the cross provides us with the most appropriate response to the powers – change, in any direction, through redemptive suffering. It is not only a response to the powers. It is also an example to the community of faith concerning its response (to the powers). Those who have been liberated by the cross are to be marked by the cross, exhibiting its example when dealing with the principalities and powers. The broad work of salvation, dealing with unrighteousness and injustice is to be tackled with the weapon of the cross. The fight is 'against the principalities, against the powers, against the world rulers of this present darkness, against the spiritual hosts of wickedness in the heavenly places'. It is the church that will engage in this warfare: 'through the church the manifold wisdom of God might now be made known to the principalities and powers in the heavenly places' (Eph 3:10; 6:12). Let us listen to Berkhof again:

All resistance and every attack against the gods of this age will be unfruitful, unless the church herself *is* resistance and attack, unless she demonstrates in her life and fellowship how men can live freed from the powers. We can only preach the manifold wisdom of God to Mammon if our life displays that we are joyfully freed from his clutches. To reject nationalism we must begin by no longer recognising in our own bosoms any difference between peoples. We shall only resist social injustice and the disintegration of community if justice and mercy prevail in our own common life and social differences have lost their power to divide. Clairvoyant and warning words and deeds aimed at the state or nation are meaningful only in so far as they spring from a church whose inner life is itself her proclamation of God's manifold wisdom to the 'Powers in the air'.[7]

Jesus calls his church, the people of God, to establish an alternative society within society, a community that is immersed in the culture but distinct from society in its life-style, values and faith. This is fundamentally, though not exclusively, a political task. Whenever the church takes this task seriously, it places itself on a collision course, as Jesus did, with all principalities and powers.

During a missionary visit to Philippi (Acts 16:11–40) the apostle Paul and his companion, Silas, released a slave girl from the control of a 'spirit of divination'. She was twice enslaved – by the spirit and by her owners who were running a thriving business based on her fortune-telling. This incident of Christian ministry – the casting out of an evil spirit – revealed that the principalities and powers are not confined to evil spirits and personal trauma. No sooner had this unfortunate girl been liberated, than her owners had the entire civic apparatus on their side. An act of compassionate service was transformed into a major civic riot! The girl's slave masters, the civil powers and the mob joined in a concerted attack against Paul and Silas. Why? Because they felt that these men and their actions threatened the very foundations of their society. The powers swung into action because this act of liberation exposed their fragile hold over those things which held Philippian society together: 'These men are Jews and they are disturbing our city. They advocate customs which it is not lawful for us Romans to accept or practice' (Acts 16:20–21).

As far as the Philippians were concerned, this was no mere incident of spiritual warfare at the personal level. It was a direct assault on their social reality, their economy, their livelihood, and their civil law and order. They reacted with vehemence and violence, bringing the full weight of the Roman power to bear on those two servants of the risen Christ, who were simply releasing the hold of the evil one over the life of an unfortunate girl.

There is no distinction of principle in the biblical record between personal and social action against the principalities and powers. Distinctions are strategic only, and depend upon the object against which the liberating action takes place, and the time and circumstance of its execution. Sometimes it is a person who is the object, sometimes it is a power. Sometimes, when the focus is upon a person, the social powers are incited into action, revealing their true nature as pretenders and usurpers.

Tackling the principalities and powers is a risky business, but it is not the same as 'political activism' in the contemporary sense. It *is* a political task, but the 'weapons of our warfare are not worldly, but have divine power to destroy strongholds'. We are called by Jesus, the divine servant, to stand against the powers with the weapon of the cross. The believer must take up his defence against the powers by standing, simply by his faith. It is not the believer's duty to bring the powers to their knees, that is Jesus' own task.[8]

This is not an encouragement to inactivity or quietism. Rather it is a call to faithfulness. We have addressed the specific social and political responses of the community of faith elsewhere in this book.[9] The presence of principalities and powers is pervasive and their impact on human creation brings a dubious blessing. We cannot do without them; they hold life together. But we cannot do with them either; they hold life away from God, and ourselves in oppression and fear. Andre Brink, in his novel about the South African experience, *A Dry White Season*, records this reflection about the pervasive power of a tyranny. Ben Du Toit, his hero, finally realises he cannot beat the system and that ultimately it has absolute power over his life:

Today I realise that this is the worst of all: that I can no longer single out my enemy and give him a name. I can't challenge him to a duel. What is set up against me is not a man, not even a group of people, but a thing, a something, a vague amorphous something, and invisible ubiquitous power that inspects my mail and taps my telephone and indoctrinates my colleagues and incites the pupils against me and cuts up the tyres of my car and paints signs on my door and fires shots into my home and sends me bombs in the mail, a power that follows me wherever I go, day and night, day and night, frustrating me, intimidating me, playing with me according to the rules devised and whimsically changed by itself.

So there is nothing I can really do, no effective counter move to execute, since I do not even know where my dark, invisible enemy is lurking or from whence he will pounce next time. And at any moment, if it pleases him, he can destroy me. It all depends solely on his fancy. He may decide that he wanted only to scare me and that he is now tired of playing with me and that in future he'll leave me alone; or he may decide that this is only the beginning, and that he is going to push me until he can have his way with me. And where and when is that?[10]

There is an answer to this chilling reality. The Christian community is called to 'put on the whole armour of God'. The cross marks the victory of Christ over the powers. The battle is over and the powers have lost! Until the final restoration of all things and the fulfilment of the kingdom, we are simply involved in the 'great skirmish'. The evil one or the powers can no longer mount a frontal attack on us. They can now employ only tricks, wiles, traps, deceit and other such subversive tactics.

The Christian disciple and the Christian community are to respond by standing firm, dressed and ready for the skirmish (Eph 6:12). Fighting such realities means having appropriate armour: truth, righteousness, the gospel of peace, faith, salvation and the word of God (Eph 6:13–18). I agree with Hendrik Berkhof that these weapons are defensive. Christ has already defeated the powers. His was the offensive. Now we are to stand and resist:

The figurative allusion to weapons points to this defensive role. Girdle, breastplate, shoes, shield, helmet and sword (*machaira*, the short sword) are all offensive arms. Lance, spear, bows and arrows are not named.[11]

These offensive weapons are now unnecessary, because Jesus has already defeated the powers.

The strife is o'er, the battle done;
Now is the Victor's triumph won;
Now be the song of praise begun: Alleluia!
The powers of death have done their worst,
But Christ their legions hath dispersed;
Let shouts of holy joy outburst: Alleluia![12]

🎇 For Reflection/Discussion

1 Read and study Isaiah 58:1–11. Can you see the link between practising compassion and doing justice on one hand and inner healing on the other? What challenge does the link between fasting and doing justice present to you?

2 Read and study Colossians 1:13–14 in the light of the following two statements:

Principalities, powers, dominions and thrones oppress, suppress, possess, deceive, control and demand allegiance. Deliverance presupposes injustice, for one does not need to be delivered from structures and realities that are just.

Salvation is about deliverance, from principalities and powers, dominions and structures that oppress and divide. The principal aim of the powers is to keep all creation and human creatures away from God, holding them together in a bond of deception. True salvation breaks this bond. It is therefore both political and personal.

3 Read and study Colossians 1:20–22 and 2:13–15 in the light of the following statement:

A doctrine of salvation that excludes, minimises or trivialises liberation from *all* principalities, powers and governing structures is bogus. Whenever the gospel is misrepresented in this way, it has to be rejected as idolatry.

How faithful is your representation of the gospel to the demand for liberation from *all* principalities and powers?

4 'Christianity is about kings and kingdoms. It is about acting at times against decrees, and about reversing the social order.' What is your reaction to this statement? Have you or has your church community ever 'acted against decrees' or taken any action to reverse the social order?

🌿 Notes

1 Coretta Scott King, *My life with Martin Luther King, Jnr*, Hodder & Stoughton, 1969, p253. Extract from the Lincoln Memorial Speech, 28 August 1963, 'I have a dream'.
2 John Howard Yoder, *The Original Revolution*, Scottdale, Penn (US): Herald Press, 1971, p18.
3 Among other documents, perhaps one of the most open espousals of this 'principal' is Peter Wagner's *Our Kind of People*.
4 John Howard Yoder, *The Politics of Jesus*, Grand Rapids, Mich (US): Wm B Eerdmans Publishing Company, 1972, p40.
5 *The Politics of Jesus*, as above, p61.
6 Hendrik Berkhof, *Christ and the Powers*, translation by John Howard Yoder, Scottdale, Penn (US): Herald Press, 1962, pp37–38.
7 *Christ and the Powers*, as above, p51.
8 I am deeply indebted to Hendrik Berkhof for his insights into the biblical teaching on 'principalities and powers', and to John Howard Yoder for his helpful translation.
9 Especially chapters 4, 5 and 6.
10 Andre Brink, *A Dry White Season*, W H Allen, 1979, p237.
11 *Christ and the Powers*, as above, p52.
12 Twelfth-century hymn, author unknown.

❀ Chapter 4 ❀

Costly Compassion and Practising Justice

The principalities have been disarmed. The powers have
been triumphed over. The process of reconciliation and restoration has begun as a result of the decisive work of Jesus
on the cross. Creation's groan is gradually begin transformed
into a song of joy and praise. The human creature is beginning to revel in a restored image and a reconciled relationship with God – a new creation in a new community
participating in a new order. 'When anyone is united to
Christ, there is a new world; the old order has gone, and a
new order has already begun' (2 Cor 5:17, NEB). Until this
process is complete, however, we continue to live in the
midst of alienation and sin in the world of creation, history
and persons. Jesus calls his followers to live in this interim
period as people of the new order in the presence of the old.
His call is to a life of service, compassion and justice: 'For
the Son of man also came not to be served but to serve, and
to give his life as a ransom for many' (Mark 10:45).

Jesus was very adept at explaining himself in profound
one-liners! He is a servant, and his mission is 'to serve'
others. Yet this simplicity speaks of a breadth of concern
that is as large and as extensive as the kingdom itself. Indeed,
the scope of the Christian community's mission is very broad.
It reflects the gospel of the kingdom, that 'kaleidoscope of
divine concern' about the whole of creation. Mission neither
begins nor ends with responsible evangelism. It includes and
goes far beyond 'doing good deeds'. The gospel of the kingdom calls Christian disciples to engage with God in the work
of change and renewal in all of creation. The cosmic scope of
salvation, the message of the kingdom as preached by Jesus,
the implications of his work, and the teaching in the Old
Testament reflecting God's concern for society, justice and
the poor, all indicate how extensive the scope of Christian
mission is.

❦ ❦ ❦

The mission of Christian disciples is modelled on Jesus. We
are sent into the world as servants, as he was sent into the
world as a servant (John 20:21b). In Mark 10:45 Jesus

describes himself as a servant redeemer. His signs and his teaching confirm this. The description in Matthew 25:31–46, of the separation of the nations (as sheep from goats) on the basis of whether they offered compassionate service 'to the least of these', indicates that Jesus placed a very high priority on compassionate service to people in need. It was the hallmark of his dealings with individuals. It follows, then, that costly compassion is an essential component of the mission for his disciples.

Jesus loved all sorts and conditions of people in need: prostitutes, Roman collaborators, Samaritans, the common people and his enemies. He physically healed the blind and the lepers; he physically fed the hungry; he liberated women, children and Samaritans from the social, political and economic scourge of being non-persons. He brought not only personal freedom, but social and political freedom as he proclaimed and embodied his own social and political alternative – the kingdom of God – which he declared was a present reality.

His miracles, healings, acts of compassion and service were all described as signs of the kingdom, which is to say they were demonstrations against all that was alien to his kingdom, where there is only justice, righteousness, love, peace and wholeness. These signs were not evangelistic visual aids especially designed to get over a spiritual point! God is not cynical about human pain, suffering and alienation. Jesus' signs were an expression of servanthood, a fulfilment of the Old Testament prophetic tradition and the words of Mary's song:

My soul magnifies the Lord,
and my spirit rejoices in God my Saviour . . .
He has shown strength with his arm,
he has scattered the proud in the imagination of their hearts,
he has put down the mighty from their thrones,
and exalted those of low degree;
he has filled the hungry with good things,
and the rich he has sent empty away.   (*Luke 1:46–47,51–53*)

No area of human need, no challenge of the powers and principalities, no experience, concern or reality and no corner of God's creation are beyond the scope of Jesus' mission. The mission of his followers is the same. Any Christian community which ignores or consistently fails to follow the example of Jesus, and hence the requirement of compassionate servanthood, disqualifies itself as an authentic Christian community. Jesus is the servant Redeemer; the church is a servant community. Its first point of contact with those in need ought *not* to be the evangelistic commando raid! Compassionate service is the contact point as well as the main conduit through which the Christian community meets the wider community. It is the obedient response to Jesus and the 'interface' between the Christian community's life and the wider world:

'I was hungry and you gave me food, I was thirsty and you gave me drink, I was a stranger and you welcomed me, I was naked and you clothed me, I was sick and you visited me, I was in prison and you came to me.' (*Matthew 25:35–36*)

This is compassionate service, urgent, immediate and affective. It involves a deliberate choice to stand with the poor and the powerless. Evangelism without costly, compassionate service is uncaring proselytism which regards 'converts' simply as evangelistic digits. Compassionate service recognises that 'hungry men have no ears'. It is service 'to the least of these', which is also done to Jesus. It is service that breaks down barriers between human sisters and brothers, some in need and others responding to that need.

In answer to the question, 'What does it mean to be here for others?', the Christian community's answer must be, 'To offer compassionate service'. Such compassionate service is not simply a theological consequence but a *fruit* of our discipleship. Mission is not a commodity to be worn as an outer garment, it is an extension of the personality. Compassionate service is extending to others our experience of the grace of caring community.

And so, without question, we will wash dirty feet, care for the diseased, include the foreigner and the marginalised, and break down in our hearts and relationships – both within and outside the Christian community – any hostility to other races, peoples, classes and the opposite sex. We will reach out in love to our enemies, lift up the little people and make sure that no fellow image-bearers suffer because we have failed to respond to their need. Yes, we shall do all that and more as we are challenged to. Finally, if necessary, we shall lay down our lives for our friends. And ask nothing in return.

∽ ∽ ∽

However, philanthropy is not enough. Compassion is the

fundamental and primary response of the Christian community; but after the hungry have been fed, the naked clothed, the widow and the fatherless defended, and the poor cared for, we must ask the question 'Why?' Why are the hungry starving, the poor poor, the naked unclothed and the stranger excluded from a place in the sun? The answers to these questions drive us to deal with the causes of evil and not simply with its consequences. Compassion is our response to the results of evil. Justice tackles its root causes.

Some branches of the Christian community insist on the fundamental priority of 'evangelism' (as they define it), which makes the matter of justice a secondary and most often an optional Christian responsibility. We have said enough to show that this is a fallacious position. It is based on the mistaken view that the gospel is words and, as a consequence, evangelism is primarily the process of proclaiming those words. Further, although this is a fundamental evangelical tenet, there is not a single biblical statement that specifies this priority. When scripture as a whole is taken into consideration, this view is further weakened. It becomes clear that God takes the matter of justice extremely seriously indeed, making it a personal preoccupation. It is as if while handing out 'portfolios' to others, God has personally retained the superintendency of this one.

Whatever the biblical focus, whether praise, trust, covenant, piety, fasting, prayer, celebration, jurisprudence, government, the Messiah's coming, liberation, forgiveness, health or obedience, the passionate concern of God for the poor and the oppressed shines through. Here are a few samples. In Psalm 146:1,6–9 the focus is on praise and trust:

Praise the Lord!
Praise the Lord, O my soul! . . .
who made heaven and earth,
    the sea, and all that is in them;
who keeps faith for ever;
    who executes justice for the oppressed;
    who gives food to the hungry.

The Lord sets the prisoners free;
    the Lord opens the eyes of the blind.
The Lord lifts up those who are bowed down;
    the Lord loves the righteous.
The Lord watches over the sojourners,
    he upholds the widow and the fatherless;
    but the way of the wicked he brings to ruin.

God is the champion of the oppressed, the defender of the poor and needy, and the executor of justice for the oppressed. How can God's people relegate this passionate divine concern to a secondary place in mission?

In Psalm 15 the focus is on piety:

O Lord, who shall sojourn in thy tent?
    Who shall dwell on thy holy hill?

The psalmist's questions are urgent and important. Who may experience intimacy with God? His answer packs a surprise:

He who walks blamelessly, and does what is right,
    and speaks truth from his heart;
who does not slander with his tongue,
    and does no evil to his friend,
        nor takes up a reproach against his neighbour . . .
who swears to his own hurt and does not change;
who does not put out his money at interest,
    and does not take a bribe against the innocent.

In other words, piety is not about a religious or mystical response to God, it is about an ethical life that demonstrates love for God as we do what is right by our neighbour.

In Isaiah 58 the focus is on fasting:

Behold, in the day of your fast you seek your own pleasure,
    and oppress all your workers.
Behold, you fast only to quarrel and to fight
    and to hit with wicked fist.
Fasting like yours this day
    will not make your voice to be heard on high.
Is such the fast that I choose,
    a day for a man to humble himself?
Is it to bow down his head like a rush,
    and to spread sackcloth and ashes under him?
Will you call this a fast,
    and a day acceptable to the Lord?

Is not this the fast that I choose:
    to loose the bonds of wickedness,
    to undo the thongs of the yoke,
to let the oppressed go free, and to break every yoke?
Is it not to share your bread with the hungry,
    and bring the homeless poor into your house;
when you see the naked, to cover him,
        and not to hide yourself from your own flesh?
. . . if you pour yourself out for the hungry
    and satisfy the desire of the afflicted,
then shall your light rise in the darkness . . .

A life of compassion and justice is described here as the fast that pleases God. Interestingly, the rest of the passage indicates that this is also the means of obtaining personal peace, fulfilment and a relationship with God, the Just.

Elsewhere in the Old Testament there are further glimpses of this passionate divine preoccupation with justice:

... I cannot endure iniquity and solemn assembly ...
When you spread forth your hands,
   I will hide my eyes from you;
even though you make many prayers,
   I will not listen;
   your hands are full of blood.
Wash yourselves; make yourselves clean;
   remove the evil of your doings from before my eyes;
cease to do evil,
   learn to do good;
seek justice,
   correct oppression;
defend the fatherless
   plead for the widow.   (*Isaiah 1:13,15–17*)

Take away from me the noise of your songs;
   to the melody of your harps I will not listen.
But let justice roll down like waters,
   and righteousness like an ever-flowing stream.
         (*Amos 5:23,24*)

Religious ritual divorced from moral righteousness is totally unacceptable to the God of justice. In fact, the *only* praise and celebration acceptable is that which issues from people whose common life reflects God's concern for the poor and oppressed.

Acceptable praise and celebration is that celebration of justice that rolls on like rivers, and of righteousness that flows relentlessly on like a perpetual stream. There is an intoxicating vigour about communities that celebrate the goodness and justice of God through a common life committed to this divine preoccupation. It may well be that the God of justice responds to the praise and celebration of most Western churches in the same way in which he responded to his ancient people – with the hidden face and blocked ears, offended by celebration that is not linked to a common life of caring and the practice of justice.

In the following verses from Isaiah and Proverbs, the focus is on government and jurisprudence:

How the faithful city has become a harlot,
    she that was full of justice!
    Righteousness lodged in her,
    but now murderers.
Your silver has become dross,
    your wine mixed with water.
Your princes are rebels
    and companions of thieves.
Everyone loves a bribe
    and runs after gifts.
They do not defend the fatherless,
    and the widow's cause does not come to them.
                    (Isaiah 1:21–23)

By justice a king gives stability to the land,
    but one who exacts gifts ruins it . . .
If a king judges the poor with equity
    his throne will be established for ever.
                    (Proverbs 29:4,14)

These verses indicate that the fundamental purpose of government is to defend the poor and powerless. A society's worth is to be measured not by its gross national product (GNP), or its gross domestic product (GDP), its wealthiest two hundred, its balance of payments surplus, its fine monuments, its architecture or its art, pleasing and praiseworthy though these may be. In the end, the measure by which a society ought to be judged has to be its treatment of its most unfortunate and powerless members.

In Isaiah chapters 9 and 11, the focus is on the coming of the messianic King – God's answer to the problem of personal, structural and cosmic evil in creation. This King will rule with justice and, not surprisingly, is an advocate for the poor:

For to us a child is born,
    to us a son is given;
and the government will be upon his shoulder,
    and his name will be called
'Wonderful Counsellor, Mighty God,
    Everlasting Father, Prince of Peace.'
Of the increase of his government and of peace
    there will be no end,
upon the throne of David, and over his kingdom,
    to establish it, and to uphold it
with justice and with righteousness
    from this time forth and for evermore.
                    (Isaiah 9:6,7)

And the Spirit of the Lord shall rest upon him,
  the spirit of wisdom and understanding,
  the spirit of counsel and might,
  the spirit of knowledge and the fear of the Lord.
And his delight shall be in the fear of the Lord.

He shall not judge by what his eyes see,
  or decide by what his ears hear;
but with righteousness he shall judge the poor,
  and decide with equity for the meek of the earth ...
                                                    (*Isaiah 11:2–4*)

These few biblical examples show that a concern for justice is not simply the preserve of the 'loony-left'. Neither is it some theologically unsound place occupied by Christians who have lost their (evangelical) way. Nor is it of consequential, marginal or secondary concern to God. Justice is central to the divine enterprise. And this is only the tip of the biblical iceberg. Not too far below the surface lies a wealth of divine concern for the poor and the powerless.

We conclude where we began; justice is a personal preoccupation of God. This is why it has to be a preoccupation for God's people. Oppressing the poor and denying the oppressed justice are not simply unfortunate violations of human rights. They are an affront to God. Nothing raises the ire of a holy God more than this damage to 'the least of these':

He who oppresses a poor man insults his Maker.
  but he who is kind to the needy honours him.

He who oppresses the poor to increase his own wealth,
  or gives to the rich, will only come to want.
                                              (*Proverbs 14:31; 22:16*)

If the matter is so clear and conclusive, why then is it such a focus of contention within the Christian community? I suggest two reasons.

First, there is a fundamental misunderstanding of the very nature of justice. Justice is most often seen as distributive – a human right or, in other words, 'to each equally'. Conversely, justice is seen as retributive – a reward or punishment or, in other words, 'to each as each has earned'. However, the biblical vision of justice is restorative – a divine gift or, in other words, 'what each needs'. In a word – grace.

This misunderstanding of the nature of justice arises because it is seen principally as a lofty human ideal rather than a divine grace. If justice is an expression of the very character of God, then the Christian community cannot regard it as optional. If, on the other hand, it is a lofty human ideal, then it can quite easily be shifted to a peripheral position in our discipleship. Restorative justice, however, is a divine preoccupation. It must also be ours.

It was restorative justice that liberated the ancient nation of Israel from the oppression in Egypt, not because they were anything special but because they needed such justice. It was this restorative justice that was overseeing the migration of the ancient Ethiopians and Philistines. This restorative justice protected the Moabite outcasts, and was constantly put into action within the nation of Israel on behalf of the widow, the orphan, the stranger and the landless poor, because they needed it. Not because they earned it, nor because they deserved it or demanded it, but because they needed it. This restorative justice comes to those in need because of God's grace – divine kindness to needy humans.

This leads us to the second reason why this matter of justice is a contentious question to many Christians. We referred earlier to the Western church's tendency to 'dichotomise the complementary' by driving an almost indestructible wedge between things that belong together. This tendency has caused some branches of the church to conclude that justification is primary and that justice is secondary. But here is yet another fallacy. Thankfully, the apostle James dealt with this one almost nineteen hundred years ago:

What does it profit, my brethren, if a man says he has faith but has not works? Can his faith save him? If a brother or sister is ill-clad and in lack of daily food, and one of you says to them, 'Go in peace, be warmed and filled,' without giving them the things needed for the body, what does it profit? So faith by itself, if it has no works, is dead.

But some one will say, 'You have faith and I have works.' Show me your faith apart from your works, and I by my works will show you my faith. (*James 2:14–18*)

Or, to paraphrase:

But someone will say, 'You prioritise faith and I prioritise works. You prioritise justification and I prioritise justice. Show me your justification apart from your justice and I by my works of justice will demonstrate to you that I have been justified.'

The truth is that faith and works belong together. So do restorative justice and justification. They are two inseparable sides of the one coin – grace – not two choices in hierarchical relationship. Justice and justification are companions, not combatants. And grace is where justice and justification meet.

❧ ❧ ❧

To use another picture, grace, justice and justification are like three sides of a triangle which provide the framework for the salvation work of the kingdom of God. This framework is celebrated in the Old and the New Testaments. The Old Testament is the backdrop of the unfolding drama of God's redemption work. The law, the wisdom literature and especially the prophets provide us with ample evidence that the covenant community was a context for the practice of justice. In other words, the drama of redemption and the practice of justice find a common focus in the unfolding of the work of the kingdom of God which is the work of grace.

At the pivotal points of God's dealings with people, this framework of grace, justice and justification is evident. For example, the giving of the ten commandments marks the first of God's agreements (the covenant) with the liberated Israelite slaves. These commandments and the rest of the law are predicated upon the assertion that the God of the covenant is a liberator dispensing restorative justice: 'I am the Lord your God who brought you out of the land of Egypt, out of the house of bondage'. This is the basis of the covenant – justification flowing out of restorative justice. This is God's grace – divine kindness to those needy (Israelite) humans, not because they deserved it, earned it or demanded it, but because they needed it and God the Just acted for them.

The year of jubilee – that fiftieth year festival of justice, freedom and equalisation within the nation of Israel – began on the Day of Atonement. This day was set aside for Israel to make appropriate amends for her sin. It was on this day of justification that captives were released, the oppressed liberated and the indebted exonerated. This was indeed good news to the poor. It was the day on which the acceptable year of the Lord, the year of jubilee, began. God was saying, in effect, 'Israel, I have this day forgiven your debts. You do the same to your fellows within the covenant community.' Here again is that union of grace, justice and justification.

The Lord's Prayer puts this framework of grace, justice and justification clearly, succinctly and beyond question for us: 'And forgive us our debts, as we also have forgiven our debtors' (Matt 6:12). Matthew's postscript puts it even more uncompromisingly: 'For if you forgive men their trespasses, your heavenly Father also will forgive you; but if you do not forgive men their trespasses, neither will your Father forgive your trespasses' (v14). Grace provides the framework for justice and justification. One is impossible without the other. This framework shatters the dichotomies, clears up the misunderstandings and directs the Christian community towards its mission of costly compassion and doing justice.

When salvation is seen in this light, when the kingdom's work is recognised as so all-embracing and cohesive, when grace is seen not simply as inclusive of justice and justification but as their very *expression*, then the church's mission will be understood as a kingdom work in which the practice of justice is central. Such a vision compels our attention and calls for our allegiance, revealing to us the character of God as one who is just and who keeps the agreement (covenant). Within the covenant community no one could possess another, oppress another, or enslave another. For to do so would be an insult, dishonouring the God of the covenant and denying the liberation (from Egyptian slavery).

The purpose of the Covenant was to celebrate the salvation of God, especially within the context of a new nationhood where personal relationships and social realities would no longer be regulated by the dictates of the slave economy but by a covenant based upon the character of a God who is just. In this light, it is not surprising that Mary's song of praise (Luke 1:46–55) and Jesus' manifesto (Luke 4:18–19) should signal the coming of the Redeemer as an occasion for a fundamental rearrangement of social priorities based on the simple but profound notion that the God who saves people from their sins is a God of justice.

❧ ❧ ❧

So, what does all this mean for the action of the church? If justice for humans is God's passion, then that should be reflected in our every thought and action, passion and desire. If it is, justice will find prominence on any and every agenda of God's people. It will not be relegated to a secondary or optional place on the agenda of discipleship. It will be the primary and most prominent consequence of the outpouring of the Holy Spirit.

Evangelicals have had 'decades of evangelism'. We have organised large, world-wide congresses on evangelisation.

We have had renewal weeks, conferences on revival and international conferences on the outpouring of the Spirit. There are several magazines dedicated to issues of charismatic renewal, church growth, healing and, so it seems, every concern under the sun. Yet not once in living memory have we had even a 'Year of Justice', let alone a decade. I have attended many conferences over twenty years, yet there has never been an international evangelical event entitled, say, 'Let justice roll down', where the main theme explored was the biblical call to the Christian community to do works of justice and costly compassion. In fact, many of us who see the issue of justice as central to the message of salvation have had to argue the case strongly with organisers even to get this theme included on their agenda. And then it has often been relegated to second-line seminars and electives (for those inclined to this minority interest!), while the main event concentrates on the 'really important' matters.

No, we haven't yet had that main event on justice, with topics like 'Justice and church growth' or 'Has evangelism any place in pursuing justice and compassion?' or 'Justice and inner healing'. (There is a whole seminar on this one based on Isaiah 58, verses 6 to 11, for example!)

In mentioning that such an event hasn't yet been held, I am simply illustrating that the theme of justice is not important enough to contemporary evangelical popular culture to warrant serious attention. This is evident also in evangelical literature. Authors who write on this theme often have their evangelical credentials questioned. They may be regarded as 'not anointed'. With a very few exceptions, books on the theme are consigned to the shelves for unpopular or 'boring' material in Christian bookshops, while the latest offerings on inner healing (largely for over-catered-for Westerners) and the latest crazes for blessing-seekers sell in their thousands. This is a harsh criticism, but in my opinion not unjustified. We forget that God has reserved the strongest possible divine criticism for worship that is not the fruit of a life characterised by the practice of justice and costly compassion: 'I cannot endure iniquity and solemn assembly . . . When you spread forth your hands, I will hide my eyes from you; even though you make many prayers, I will not listen . . . seek justice, correct oppression; defend the fatherless, plead for the widow' (Isa 1:13,15–17).

When our strategies for justice emerge, matching in every way the plethora of already existing strategies for evangelism, church growth, healing, times of refreshing, and so on, then we shall know for certain that we have been captured by this passion of God. When our worship, prayers and songs in every church, Bible study and small group in every town, city and village reverberate to the strains of justice rolling down like waters and righteousness like an ever-flowing stream, then we shall know for certain that justice is as important as any of our other concerns. When disciples – old and especially the young – begin to respond in *droves* to care for the poor and to work for justice and ecological responsibility globally, then we shall know for certain that this passion of God has captured the church.

Micah's summary of the matter is both eloquent and irresistible:

He has showed you, O man, what is good;
    and what does the Lord require of you
but to do justice, and to love kindness,
    and to walk humbly with your God?
(Micah 6:8)

❧ *For Reflection/Discussion*

1 Do you agree that justice is a preoccupation of God, as I have outlined in this chapter?

2 'Grace is where justice and justification meet.' Is this true? Would you expect evangelistic messages to reflect this?

    Construct an evangelistic message to a group of disadvantaged youth in a big city, for example Liverpool, that would convey to them God's concern for their situation.

3 'The poor you will have with you always.' Would you say that this statement of Jesus was a prediction ('prophecy') or an observation on the effects of human greed and injustice?

4 Has the revolution in worship in our churches – as demonstrated by the explosion of interest in new worship songs, ministry and the many 'manifestations' – been matched by an equal explosion of concern and action for justice by churches? Evaluate this in the light of Amos 5:21–24 and Isaiah 1:13–18.

❧ Chapter 5 ❧

Christian Social Responsibility

'But woe to you Pharisees! for you tithe mint and rue and every herb, and neglect justice and the love of God . . .' (*Luke 11:42*)

'These men who have turned the world upside down have come here also . . . and they are all acting against the decrees of Caesar, saying that there is another king, Jesus.' (*Acts 17:6–7*)

These two passages are significant. The first warns us, as it did the Pharisees, of the danger of legalistic hypocrisy coupled with indifference to justice. The second draws on the experience of the early Christians, laying out the mission agenda of Jesus' followers in sharp and socially confrontational terms. If we take the kingdom seriously, there will be upheaval in the social order and a radical change of allegiances. The only reason why this is not obvious to the contemporary church, especially in the West, is because of captivity to a particular culture. Western churches do not see themselves as being in captivity because they are blinded by the immense privileges that they enjoy in Western society. Consequently, they tend to keep quite about rampant injustices that are part of the fabric of the societies on which they depend for support. Such churches cannot claim that Jesus alone is Lord. This is one of the reasons why Julian Fisher left:

My final reason for leaving the church concerns the artificiality, exclusiveness and irrelevance of the institution as perceived by an onlooker. In too many churches there is a lack of robustness of purpose, a reluctance to speak out to the wider community on issues that are crucial to the *here and now world* in which we find ourselves. Too little unanimity of voice as an alternative to the mainstream; too much silence and therefore acquiescence for fear of 'rocking the boat'. The church is usually seen as a club . . . for society's weaklings – boring, smug, self-satisfied and irrelevant to the real needs and questions facing people's lives.

Strong stuff, Julian, but with more than a grain of truth.

Julian has joined the refugees. When he told me so recently, I was deeply saddened and asked him to write down his reasons for me. He prefaced them with these eloquent words:

It is with profound mourning and regret that I find myself alienated from the organisation known as the church ... From a joyful, euphoric and mentally challenging experience which I confidently identified as the 'born again' renewal of my nature by the Holy Spirit, I felt and believed in grateful humility that God had seen fit to bless me with the elusive *truth* about life and the way to live it. *Twenty years on I remain convinced of the efficacy of that event!*

And yet we have lost him. Had we been truly faithful to our creed, and prophetic in our words and actions in the contemporary world, Julian would have continued to throw in his passionate lot with us. However, now, in order to maintain the integrity of his faith, he has to find other ways to live out his 'born again' experience. We may disagree with his action, as I do. However, his eloquence, in reason and passion, calls for our response.

If Julian had seen a few things more consistently, he might have stayed. First, he needed to experience a 'servant community', serving its fellow human beings with sacrifice and without expectation, thus creating conditions under which they would want to become followers and disciples of Jesus. Compassionate service brings people together on a level footing. It breaks down barriers. It illustrates the old adage, 'Beggars help other beggars to find bread'. Nothing breaks down barriers more than a 'leper' being hugged, a cup of cold water for the thirsty, food for a starving child, intelligence and know-how that enables a community to break free from dependence on the 'charity' of others and into that place where they can help themselves. This is the power given to people by God.

Second, Julian might have stayed if he experienced a community that spread the fragrance and the illumination of Christ. In relating to what Julian called the here and now world, there is a need for judgement without condemnation, for truth-telling without arrogance, for teaching with empathy and understanding, and proclamation of the gospel in weakness rather than triumphalism.

Third, unconditional love: Julian's background, which he described as typical of many others, was one in which 'unconditional love was not much in evidence ... I sincerely believed both on an intellectual and heartfelt spiritual level that the body of believers would become the family of acceptance which Jesus seemed to promise.' What a tragedy! Maybe his expectations were unrealistic, but he was constantly appealing to the principles of scripture against which he measured his expectations. We need to love in such a way that the community of faith is a showcase for the kingdom of God. Julian was and continues to be a giver. His departure is a sad loss.

$$\mathcal{eg} \;\; \mathcal{eg} \;\; \mathcal{eg}$$

We have said that *compassion* is the fundamental and primary response of the Christian community in the face of human need. It deals with the *consequences* of evil. We have also said that *justice* is the divine preoccupation. It therefore is a central Christian responsibility and deals with the causes of evil.

The two verses that introduce this chapter make it clear that mission has to do with practising justice, altering allegiances and initiating massive social rearrangements. As indicated in Mary's song of praise, this means scattering the proud, putting down the mighty from their thrones, lifting up the little people, filling the hungry with good things and sending the rich empty away. This kind of mission produces a new community, where the last will be first and the great the servant of all (Mark 10:42–45), where the meek, not the powerful, will inherit the earth, and where the outcast and the marginalised, the lame, the blind and the crippled will be honoured guests in the kingdom community.

This is the stuff of the church's mission – revolutionary stuff! This is why so many Western Christians regard it as dispensable rhetoric. To accept this as the mission programme of the people of God would automatically set most Western churches on a collision course with the source of their privileges and creature comforts – and most of their members, too. Accepting this programme, however, would end our cultural captivity. It would reinstate Jesus as Lord of the church and restore to us the privilege of being a kingdom community.

This programme catapults the Christian community into the struggle for justice against the principalities and powers, those hidden structures of human existence. In oppression, alienation and injustice they hold society together in a fragile peace while at the same time holding it away from God the Just, because society oppresses God's needy children. The Christian message must address itself to the predicament of humanity, and the Christian community must apply its mission to putting things right in contemporary society. This means tackling the root causes of evil. It means engagement with the structures and forces of evil that cause injustice. This is the social responsibility of Christian disciples, an indispensable component of the work of mission.

ₑₒ ₑₒ ₑₒ

We have witnessed a transition in the arena of social protest and in the struggle for social change since the 1960s. Then idealism and romanticism motivated the disciples of the 'new age' that was coming. It was idealism which motivated the anti-war protests and the desire for peace. It was romanticism which inspired the vision to 'live more simply that others may simply live'.

Nowadays, however, the situation has changed from altruism to survival. Peace is now a matter of necessity, because the system of nuclear deterrence, supposedly there for our security, also represents the potential for the most terrible end of life on this planet at any time. Furthermore, ecology is now a matter of survival. The crisis that we face is what writer Jurgen Moltmann has called 'the ecological death of nature and the ecological suicide of humanity'.[1] Our rape and mistreatment of the earth, its ecosystems and its resources have meant that humanity is now fatally threatened by itself. We are planning and executing our own extinction! We find ourselves caught between two self-inflicted courses of potential destruction. As Moltmann has also said, 'A nuclear war is "apocalypse now", the destruction of nature is an "apocalypse by instalment".'[2]

ₑₒ ₑₒ ₑₒ

These pressing realities have led many social reformers within and beyond the church to redefine the notion of peace itself, and to rearrange the priorities for social transformation. Because of the need for survival, 'peace' is now defined almost exclusively as an absence of war and the presence of 'law and order'. Because of the need for survival, we say that we may happily live in that 'peace' which the absence of war has given us. The result of this redefinition has been to relegate the concern for justice to a secondary position because, as the argument goes, 'fighting for a world free of the threat of nuclear holocaust is the most important issue of our age. If we are all blown to bits, fighting for justice will become irrelevant. There will be no poor or oppressed people to fight for anyway!' Variations of this same logic are applied to the struggle for a green world.

But herein lies another fundamental fallacy. The pursuit of a nuclear-free 'peace' in a world where there is massive and widespread injustice and poverty has a hollow ring. The poor do not wish to live in a 'peaceful' world where millions starve and thousands die daily of malnutrition and preventable diseases, while the nuclear superpowers spend in multiples annually on arms of nuclear deterrence or on wars to protect oil supplies, the resources that are required to adequately feed and medically care for them. In such a world the rich delude themselves into thinking that they live in peace because they overlook the fact that others must, for the sake of their luxury, live in misery. Such peace is fraudulent, for it is a cloak for what Moltmann has called 'the most encompassing form of fatal violence and organised peacelessness'.

The apostle James asks the question, 'What causes wars, and what causes fighting among you?' His answer is eloquent and profound: 'You desire and do not have; so you kill. And you covet and cannot obtain; so you fight and wage war' (James 4:1,2). What he observes at the interpersonal level is also applicable at the national and international level. Covetousness, greed and envy are the causes of wars. Oppression and injustice fuel these from both sides. Inequality so often leads to violence between peoples.

If we wish to end wars, then we ought to work for and to achieve justice. Isaiah tells us that justice is the tree upon which the fruit of peace grows: 'The fruit of righteousness will be peace; the effect of righteousness will be quietness and confidence for ever' (Isa 32:17, NIV).

The principal reason for the existence of nuclear weapons and the threat of nuclear holocaust is the lack of justice in the world. It is hypocritical to declare an International Year of Peace while there is massive international injustice. It would be more appropriate to declare, even as a token, an International Year of Justice! This would at least redress the hypocritical imbalance of pursuing 'peace' at the expense of justice. This is an offence to the poor and blasphemous to God the Just. Where there is no justice, there can be no peace. Peace without justice is no peace.

It is a pity that so many concerned Christian communities seem, in their concern for peace, to have abandoned the pursuit of justice. 'Peace' and the struggle towards achieving a nuclear-free world have become the litmus paper test of radical discipleship. But the test of true discipleship is the pursuit of justice, not the witness for 'peace'. And the pressing issue of survival is not a good reason for mortgaging justice. Self-preservation is not a priority for Christian disciples. Indeed, the gospel would call us to the very opposite: to lose our lives in order to gain the kingdom.

The call of the Christian community is to pursue justice, even at the cost of our own survival. If we obeyed this call, we would be contributing significantly to the cause of peace. Justice for South African blacks, rights for the original Australians, fair trading with and aid with dignity to the two-thirds world, equality for women and for oppressed and discriminated-against minorities – to mention but a few – are all essential to the establishment of a peaceful world community.

ଓ ଓ ଓ

We have said enough to establish that peace is not simply the absence of war or conflict. It is the fruit of justice.

The Hebrew word *shalom* – that great Old Testament salvation word – expresses the true meaning of peace. For the individual, it means total humanisation and harmony with self and with all created reality. It means an integrated life with health of body, heart and mind, harmony with nature, openness to others and joy with God. Shalom leaves the recipient with the view that life is good – adequate – with nothing else to wish for. Between persons, shalom means love, mutuality and sharing, those foundations of 'community'. In society, shalom means justice, dignity, autonomy and interdependence.

Shalom is the very opposite, the very absence, of oppression, violence, suffering and selfishness. It also means the state of being a caring trustee of creation, no longer indifferent, irresponsible, or exploitative towards it. As long as people are enriching themselves at the expense of others, oppressing others, doing violence to them and terrorising them with the instruments of power, there is no shalom.

Shalom is the antidote to evil. It is a vision of each person living in fulfilment in his own house, without the fear of dispossession. It is a vision of each under his own olive tree and his own vine, of the wolf being the guest of the lamb, of the lion eating straw with the ox, of a little child leading them (Mic 4:4; Isa 11:6–9). It is a vision of the coming kingdom. This is the peace that the Christian community must work for. And its model is the Prince of Peace himself who by his cross will reconcile all things to God and restore all to their proper place and status in the creation. Peace is the heart of the message of reconciliation with God: 'He is before all things, and in him all things hold together . . . For in him all the fullness of God was pleased to dwell, and through him to reconcile to himself all things, whether on earth or in heaven, making peace by the blood of his cross' (Col 1:17, 19–20).

The cross is the heart of Christian peacemaking. Its message blazes out across time and over the social, military and imperial wrecks of history. For peace, the Prince of Peace is crucified by his enemies, freely giving his life to win theirs and to secure their peace. The cross also achieves something else: on the cross, Jesus, 'disarmed the principalities and powers and made a public example of them' (Col 2:15). Since then the principalities and powers, spiritual and temporal, hold no terror for us. Neither their nuclear arsenals nor the people against whom they are deployed for our protection hold any terror for us. We have a greater protector and another King to follow. He calls us to trust him and to be ministers of reconciliation for him in the midst of conflict.

Shalom, then, is both the absence of violence and conflict and the presence of justice. For this reason, the end of hostility in itself does not signal the presence of peace. The end of violence needs to be celebrated by equal and opposite actions of peace and justice. It is for this reason that Micah's vision of peace envisages the transformation of the weapons of warfare into agricultural implements for food production: '. . . they shall beat their swords into ploughshares, and their spears into pruning hooks; nation shall not lift up sword against nation, neither shall they learn war any more' (Mic 4:3). When the nuclear superpowers start melting down their nuclear weapons, transforming the raw materials of their arsenals and redirecting the resources of their armament industries to feed the world, then we shall know for certain that we are on the road to peace with justice. Until then we are to work for peace with justice, making certain that we do not fall into any of the following four traps:

Trap 1. The most common trap the Christian community falls into is that of *non-action in the name of piety*, on the basis that Christians should not be involved in politics. Non-action, however, is a conscious political act; it is a choice by silence to give passive support to the prevailing unjust system. This is plain disobedience to the will of God and the dictates of the kingdom. It grieves the Holy Spirit. It makes us guilty of complicity. Victor Hugo said, 'Evil triumphs when good men do nothing.'

Piety can never be a *substitute* for protest.

Trap 2. This trap is the converse – *substituting protest for piety.* There is no new and innovative solution which Christians can apply to the problems of society, including peace-making, except that which comes from the heart of God. Neither the prevailing social and political climate, nor the intensity of the issues of the moment, provide Christians with their agenda, their sustaining motivation or their wisdom in the arena of social change. Faith in God and the activity of the kingdom do.

Piety and protest are two sides of the one coin and not mutually exclusive poles on an axis. Or, to put it another way, the process for achieving peace involves prayer *and* political action.

Trap 3. This is the trap of *substituting protest against evil for the work of penetrating the kingdom of evil.* We are called to take on the world as Christ took on our human condition. The incarnation shows that there is a difference between divine protest against the world and divine penetration into the world. Protest on its own is cheap. Prophetic engagement is the next and most substantial step. This has often led Christians to lose their lives, and the church to be persecuted. For Jesus, it meant washing dirty feet, feeding the hungry, giving the thirsty drink, welcoming the stranger and fear-lessly confronting the structures of power of his day. For us, in the context of peacemaking, it means praying for peace, working for peace and transforming the world into a more just place by touching it at ground level.

Trap 4. Penetration is not the same as establishing the king-dom of God on earth. 'Thy kingdom come, thy will be done on earth as it is in heaven' is a prophetic prayer, a call to action, but not a prophecy fully realised.

As indicated by the parable of the wheat and the weeds, we must work the works of the kingdom looking to the harvest. We know that our efforts will bear some fruit of the kingdom coming but will not actually achieve today 'the kingdom come'. The weeds of evil will grow as well as the wheat of justice. We penetrate without the assurance of success. *Faithfulness*, not triumph, is our motivation.

God has made peace with us and thus transforms us into peacemakers. So we shall pray for peace, we shall work for peace, with protest, with penetration, through education, through establishing people-links internationally with allies and even with supposed 'enemies'; we shall follow the example of Jesus who recognised that 'he who is not against us is for us'.

We shall advocate peace with friends, neighbours, colleagues and governments, all the time trusting that the hostility to peace is being broken down. We shall witness for peace, even to the extent of withholding that portion of our taxes which may be spent on war, or requesting on our tax returns that this portion be used for education, overseas aid or the social services. (I acknowledge that this action may not have the desired effect, but as a device for selective civil disobedience for the kingdom's sake, it will be an effective witness for peace.)

Above all, we shall act with and place our confidence in the God who makes peace, the God and Father of our Lord Jesus Christ.

🕮 *For Reflection/Discussion*

In this chapter I have identified four traps that we may fall into as we work for peace with justice. These traps are: Pietism (non-action or substituting prayer for protest), Activism (substituting protest for prayer), Humanism (using protest as a substitute for incarnation), Utopianism (thinking that the fullness of God's kingdom can be realised in our earthly dimension).

I have suggested as an alternative that our calling to work for the fulfilment of the kingdom involves both prayer *and* political action. I have also suggested that our vision and our inspiration ought to be the worlds of our Lord's prayer, 'Thy kingdom come, thy will be done on earth as it is in heaven . . .' and that the way to achieve this is by incarnation and faithful service.

1 Assess the ministries and activities of your church community over the last twelve months. What traps have you fallen into? What specific steps/actions have you undertaken to respond to global needs? What sermons/Bible studies have *directly* addressed issues of human need and injustice? Have you had a day/night of prayer specifically for the vast human needs, in contrast to the need for evangelism?

2 Write a sermon/message that specifically challenges your fellowship to a serious and consistent response to issues of injustice. Base it on any of the following passages: Isaiah 58:1–12; Amos 5:21–24; Micah 6:6–8; Luke 1:46–56; Luke 4:16–20.

🥀 *Notes*

1 Jurgen Moltmann, 'Justice, Not Security, Creates Peace' (unpublished paper).
2 As above.

✿ Chapter 6 ✿

Engaging the Structures

This is where the rubber hits the road! To discuss is not to do. In the end, even God turned the Word into flesh who shared our experience – God became a human being. There is no substitute for incarnation and, as a Christian community, we are sent into the world as Jesus was sent, *to take on the world* as he took on our flesh and all its experience, vulnerability and hopes.

For decades modern evangelicalism has been putting out statements on the biblical call to social and political action. Some of our leading theologians have clarified what this means by calling us to engage the structures that govern our human existence and the cosmos. Beginning at the Minneapolis congress on evangelisation in 1966 through to the second Lausanne congress in Manila in 1989, a series of strident and thoughtful statements have emerged, calling us to action in the world.

In 1974 the Lausanne Covenant stated:

We affirm that God is both the Creator and the Judge of all men. We therefore should share God's concern for justice and reconciliation throughout human society and for the liberation of men from every kind of oppression ... The message of salvation implies also a message of judgement upon ever form of alienation, oppression and discrimination, and we should not be afraid to denounce evil and injustice wherever they exist.[1]

In 1989 the Manila Manifesto put out this challenge:

As we proclaim the love of God, we must be involved in loving service, and as we preach the kingdom of God, we must be committed to its demands for justice and peace ... the gospel is good news for the poor ... [2]

Over the years we have taken these concerns up *in our language*. As a result we have convinced ourselves that, because we have written and rehearsed these sentiments we have acted on them. But we still need to turn the words into active, consistent deeds of Christian discipleship. Our mission as a Christian community propels us into a costly and perpetual struggle against the principalities and powers.

We have already said that mission thrusts the Christian

community into centre stage in the struggle against the principalities and powers, those controlling but alienating structures that govern human existence. Mission is not simply transformation and responsible evangelism, not simply costly compassion, not simply *accepting* in our minds that justice is central to our discipleship. Mission is taking on the evil structures of our world and *doing* something concrete about injustice (as the churches have done something concrete about evangelism and compassion). These structures have abandoned their designated role of being servants of God for our good and have become our oppressors. We are called as a Christian community to stand and resist. The list of concrete actions is limitless. In this chapter I suggest but a few.

œ œ œ

Engaging the structures commits the church to be on the side of the poor, the oppressed and the victims of violence. The Old and the New Testaments make it quite clear that God is the God of the oppressed, the defender of the poor, the supporter of the weak, the protector of the defenceless and the refuge of the abandoned. It is God who 'executes justice for the fatherless and the widow, and loves the sojourner, giving him food and clothes' (Deut 10:18). It follows naturally that the convenant community must do the same: 'Love the sojourner therefore; for you were sojourners in the land of Egypt' (v19). It is God 'who executes justice for the oppressed; who gives food to the hungry. The Lord sets the prisoners free; the Lord opens the eyes of the blind. The Lord lifts up those who are bowed down...' (Ps 146:7–8). In the New Testament it is the poor to whom the kingdom of God belongs, together with the hungry, the weeping and the unjustly persecuted (Luke 6:17–38); it is the meek who shall inherit the earth (Matt 5:5). The apostle James reminds the rich of the miseries that await those who have gained their wealth by oppressing their workers, because the cries of the oppressed 'have reached the ears of the Lord of hosts' (James 5:1–6).

Mission is being here for others, the poor 'others' in a world of need. At the risk of labouring the point, the biblical message is quite clear. God is on the side of the poor, the oppressed and disadvantaged; so must the Christian community be in its priorities, in its choices, in its values, in its concerns, in its political allegiances, in its social initiatives, in the various ways in which its members choose to carry out their vocations and careers, in its investments and in its passion! The poor woman, man or child is our sister, our brother, our offspring. We need to look at the world through their eyes. This can only be done as we are close to them, in relationship with them and by instruction from them. Then, and then only, will our instinctive reflex reaction to any business, political or social policy be to ask, 'How does this affect my sister?', 'What impact will this decision have on my brother?', 'How will this product and its marketing in the two-thirds world affect my offspring?'

Surprisingly, some Christians are either offended by the suggestion that God is on the side of the poor or react to it with ambivalence. They object on the ground that God does not have favourites; God cannot love the poor any more than the rich. True, but that is not what is being proposed. It is rather that the scriptures teach that God is on the side of the poor and so the people of God must be also. God is on the side of the poor because no one else is. God is their defender because they are utterly defenceless. Who better to be their refuge, their judge, their friend and their liberator? Here is restorative justice in its fullness – justice for the poor simply because they are in need of it. No, God does not have favourites. It is *we*, the comfortable and affluent, who favour the rich, the powerful and the famous in preference to the poor. God calls us to switch sides.

It is time for change. Engaging the structures commits the Christian community to maintaining continuous solidarity with the poor through relationship and mutual respect. The Christian community is not here to 'do good' to the poor, like 'experts' in relation to dependent clients. The poor are our family. Our relationship with them is not hierarchical but mutual. We are fellow image bearers standing with those whose image, and therefore whose very existence, is threatened by the shackles of poverty and oppression. We stand with them because we accept the fundamental truth that while one single image bearer is oppressed, our own image is being fundamentally threatened. We stand with our poor sisters and brothers in relationship and mutual respect, so that our 'abundance at the present time should supply their want, so that their abundance may supply [our] want, that there may be equality' (2 Cor 8:14).

Solidarity, relationship and mutual respect are not simply abstract ideas, lofty sentiments for radical disciples. They are concrete choices to be made, otherwise even the praise-worthy motivation to care for the poor and oppressed can become depersonalised and dehumanising to the poor partners. One example of this is the way in which so many Western churches, aid and development agencies, and missionary societies use tear-jerking advertisements to secure dollars for their work in the two-thirds world. Kefa Sempangi, who works with orphans in Uganda, illustrates the point well:

People are replaced by projects, involvement by investment and commitment by supervision. Missionaries are sent to missionary fields by missionary boards, and they send home numbers to signify conversions. In this impersonal exchange, even the best of initiatives have dehumanising consequences.[3]

While visiting churches in Canada, from which most mission-aries to Uganda came, Kefa was struck by the pictures of naked Africans tacked onto bulletin boards. One of them, of a fugitive woman with her three emaciated children, made a deep impression on him. Upon his return to Uganda he located the woman, only to find that her children were still dressed in rags; one of them had a huge sore on her leg. Her picture had been used but she had been forgotten. She was just an illustrative digit in the compassion industry! This kind of exploitation is widespread and it must be stopped. This is why it is necessary to heed the call of mission, to maintain solidarity with the poor through relationships and mutual respect.

ৎও ৎও ৎও

Engaging the structures calls us to be advocates for the voiceless, in partnership with them. In the complex web that is human life, in the interweaving pattern that is human history, while others languish in life's hollow, clearly some stand on the higher ground of privilege and power. Their privileged position, however, confers on them principally not ease and complacent thankfulness but responsibility for those in the hollow.

We are to be advocates for the voiceless because it is a human duty: 'I *am* my brother's keeper'. Community is a blessing of creation because it is an expression of the character of God. To remain silent or inactive in the face of human need, is to deny the very essence of our humanity and to offend deeply the God whose image we bear.

We are to be advocates for the voiceless because we live in a global village. We live today in a global context of complex and intricate social and economic relationships. Every action, inaction or interaction has significant and, at times, far-reaching consequences. By our advocacy, or the lack of it, we contribute to these consequences.

We are to be advocates for the voiceless because to be silent is to be complicit with the evil that has enslaved them. It was Daniel Berrigan who said, 'Hatred is not the opposite of love; indifference is.'[4]

In his parable of Lazarus and the rich man (Luke 16:19–31), Jesus warns of the serious consequences of indifference in the face of evil. There is no indication that the rich man had done anything to cause Lazarus' suffering. He was simply indifferent to it:

The rich man was guilty, however, because he ignored the beggar at his gate, did nothing about his destitution, failed to use his affluence to relieve the poor man's need, and acquiesced in a situation of gross economic inequality which had dehumanised Lazarus and which he could have remedied ... Dives went to hell not because he exploited Lazarus, but because of his scandalous indifference and apathy. (*John Stott*)[5]

The experience of millions of exploited people today is rooted in a history of slavery, colonialism and Christian mission. This history underlies the current relationship between rich developed nations and all other nations of the two-thirds world. For example, the rich in Britain will celebrate the time of the founding of the British Empire as a time of its greatest glory, and they remember their forebears as 'great' men, landowners, discoverers, great colonisers, and missionaries – good people with a mission to do good to others. In fact, this particular time was characterised by some of the most horrific acts of brutality in the history of the human race. With a very few exceptions, these 'great' men did not fight for justice for others, but denied it to them. Their wealth and power were acquired not through hard work, industry and sacrifice, but through stealth, trickery and oppression.[6]

Today we are the inheritors of the wealth and achievements of that period. If these are to be celebrated, so also must the crimes, the oppression and the barbarity. The rich and powerful today cannot separate themselves from the experiences and actions of their celebrated forebears. Those actions have created the voiceless. To be silent is to give passive support to the system which has created, and which sustains, this human tragedy.

Consequently, the first action of advocacy is confession and repentance towards the poor and to the God of the poor. The creation is fallen. Evil in our world is pervasive. We are all, either by inheritance, by involvement or as beneficiaries, participants in the institutionalised evil implicit in national and international economic and trading relationships. These unjust relationships, set up during periods of colonial dominance, have been carefully crafted to maintain a relationship between the rich and the poor nations that naturally favours the rich. Land needed to grow food for the hungry had been hoarded into large estates and used to grow coffee, tea, sugar, tobacco, bananas, beef and other luxuries (Westerners call them necessities) for export to the rich.

Poor developing nations are feeding the affluent minority!
Astonishingly, since 1955, every year the rich developed nations
have imported approximately twice as many dollars worth of food
from the poor, developing nations as they exported to them.
(*Ronald Sider*)[7]

This powerful, faceless and unjust system, which continues to create more poor and to maintain them in a state of voicelessness, has turned us all into silent and compliant collaborators. We need to repent with words and actions that will restore to us the freedom of community with our voiceless sisters and brothers, and bring us the forgiveness and the grace of God the Just.

The next action of advocacy is to speak the truth about ourselves and to work towards massive and fundamental changes in our behaviour. Our advocacy at this point is not to act as self-appointed mouthpieces for the benighted poor and oppressed; they can most eloquently speak for themselves. We have to confess for ourselves.

When we have taken these steps, then we may speak together with the voiceless in true partnership as we challenge the powerful with the plea, 'Let my people go!'

❧ ❧ ❧

Engaging the structures is a call to direct action. Jesus cleansed the temple of traders. It was a deliberate, premeditated act. Zeal consumed him. He made a whip of cords himself. Then, in righteous anger, he drove them out, brandishing the whip as he went, turning over the tables, scattering the money, releasing the birds and animals. This people already had a temple and a covenant. How could they deny the Gentiles a place under the sun by turning the Court of the Gentiles – the house of prayer for all nations – into a place for cheating and swindling, a money-making marketplace for themselves? No small wonder that Jesus resorted to direct action. A den of thieves cannot be tolerated in the house of prayer for all nations, or indeed in any other place.

Direct action is, I believe, a call to cleanse the 'temple' of contemporary society of 'the den of thieves' and turn it into 'a house of prayer' for the 'others', the poor others in a world of need. So without going into the specific mechanics of direct action for every occasion (this book is not a manual for revolution), it may simply be adequate to state here that direct action is part of the Christian response to those in need.

The excesses and the exploitative employment practices of multinational corporations, the international debt crisis, the continuing inequalities of the present world economic order based as it is on unfair and inequaitable trading arrangements between rich and poor nations, the plight of political prisoners under tyrannical regimes of all political colours are all legitimate targets for 'the whip of cords'. We must fashion it ourselves and use it as Jesus did, not to express vindictiveness but to exercise correction.

The specific actions will vary and will be guided in every case by Jesus' non-vindictive example. Christians may never agree on the actual means or strategies for direct action, no more than they agree on strategies for evangelism. However, as they are all agreed on the need for evangelism, there ought to be no question about our common commitment to direct action against injustice. Prayer, prophecy, protest, 'people power', political pressure, civil disobedience, economic boycotts, education for the poor, co-operative businesses, grass-roots enterprises, credit-based and other income generation schemes among the poor, worker-controlled business enterprises, social analysis, effective social and political organisation of the oppressed, and participation in government are all part of the wide range of initiatives open to the Christian community on mission as it engages in direct action with the poor and oppressed.

The contemporary Christian community must be careful not to occupy the 'Gentiles' court', turning it into a mammon-worshipping, money-making and ease-inducing 'den of thieves' with its consumer evangelisation, its prosperity doctrines, its 'you can do it' New Age philosophies, its 'health, wealth and success' perversion of Christianity. The 'whip of cords' may well be used against us, because all these things keep the poor and the powerless, whether across the street or across the world, in their place.

Engaging the structures, then, causes us to take the side of the poor, to express solidarity with them through relationship and mutual respect, to act as advocates for the voiceless and to be involved in direct action for justice.

ꗥ ꗥ ꗥ

Mission commits the Christian community to a continuous task of watching the state! The powers that be are set in their proper place by God:

> Let every person be subject to the governing authorities. For there is no authority except from God, and those that exist have been instituted by God. Therefore he who resists the authorities resists what God has appointed, and those who resist will incur judgement. For rulers are not a terror to good conduct, but to bad. Would you have no fear of him who is in authority? Then do what is good, and you will receive his approval, for he is God's servant for your good. But if you do wrong, be afraid, for he does not bear the sword in vain; he is the servant of God to execute his wrath on the wrongdoer. (*Romans 13:1-4*)

This passage has too often been used by the powerful to beat the 'weak' into quiet submission. It has also been an inspiration to many Christians who, through apathy, lethargy or fear, have decided that it is none of their business to challenge any existing structures. Far from being a call to quietness and compliance, however, this passage is a call to vigilance! The call is to be subject to an authority whose boundaries of jurisdiction are clearly laid out. We need pay heed not only to the call to be subject but also to the context within which the call is issued. According to this passage, the proper role of authority is threefold: to exercise proper positive sanctions against bad conduct (v3); to approve good conduct (v3); to be God's servant for the common good (v4). The Christian community has a duty to maintain a watching brief over the state so as to make sure that the boundaries of its jurisdiction are adhered to. This is the universal task of the Christian community. It does not apply only to those who have the luxury of living in a liberal democracy. When the state transgresses its boundaries, it institutionalises violence, deprives the poor of their place in the sun and terrorises those who resist it in any way. There are clear biblical condemnations of such status that 'fame mischief by statute'.

Woe to those who make unjust laws,
   to those who issue oppressive decrees,
to deprive the poor of their rights
   and withhold justice from the oppressed of my people,
making widows their prey
   and robbing the fatherless.   (*Isaiah 10:1–2, NIV*)

Can a corrupt throne be allied with you –
   one that brings on misery by its decrees?
They band together against the righteous
   and condemn the innocent to death.
                    (*Psalm 94:20,21*)

Governments which enforce racist laws, or kill thousands of their own people, or terrorise those who desire justice and a place under the sun, have to be confronted and directed back within the proper boundaries of their jurisdiction.

Assuming that this insight from Romans 13:1–4 comes to us from the pen of the apostle Paul, it would be very instructive to see how he applied it. The narrative of his ministry in Philippi (see Acts 16:11–40), describing the civil disruption that it caused, his imprisonment and subsequent release and the way in which he dealt with the authorities, gives us a helpful insight into what it means for the Christian and the Christian community to 'be subject'.

On that occasion the Roman government had abused its power and transgressed the boundaries of legitimate authority by breaking its own laws, for, as Paul says, 'They have beaten us publicly, uncondemned, men who are Roman citizens, and have thrown us into prison' (Acts 16:37). This was imprisonment without trial coupled with torture. While they were in prison:

... about midnight Paul and Silas were praying and singing hymns to God, and the prisoners were listening to them, and suddenly there was a great earthquake, so that the foundations of the prison were shaken; and immediately all the doors were opened and every one's fetters were unfastened. (*Acts 16:25–26*)

Faced with the total breakdown of their penal system brought about by this act of 'divine vandalism', the authorities added insult to Paul's injury by attempting a secret release. His reaction was firm, confrontational and responsible: '... do they now cast us out secretly? No! let them come themselves and take us out' (v37). We are told that the magistrates 'came and apologised to them. And they took them out and asked them to leave the city. So they went out of the prison, and visited Lydia; and when they had seen the brethren, they exhorted them and departed' (vv39,40).

This is how we are to 'be subject', not with cowering servitude or compliant acquiescence but with confrontational responsibility. Whenever possible and wherever necessary we must call the ruling authorities back to their rightful role of dispensing government with justice and serving God for the common good. We may not always be as successful as Paul was in Philippi. The ruling authorities do not readily apologise to victims (at least not until thirty years after their death!). So we must 'stand' and 'resist' even at the cost of our own lives – death on a cross – where we know Christ has already defeated the powers, disarmed them and, ever since, has been calling them to their rightful place and purpose, anticipating that day when the kingdom of the world finally becomes the kingdom of our Lord and of his Christ (Rev 11:15). The Christian community is called to practise love, and the state to dispense justice. Vigilence and application are required in both cases. It is the vision of the kingdom that challenges us and inspires us to watch the state.

Christian social responsibility throws the Christian community into sharp and direct conflict with the adversaries of the poor. Conflict operates on the 'law of retaliation': 'an eye for an eye and a tooth for a tooth'. Within this context one inevitably becomes an enemy to the enemy, locked in the vicious cycle of evil justifying evil. Jesus replaced the 'law of retaliation' with the 'law of love for the enemy': 'Love your enemies and pray for those who persecute you' (Matt 5:44). Jesus rejected the options of retaliatory violence and quiet compliance; so must we. He chose instead to witness to the kingdom and to suffer as a minister of reconciliation. In any arena of conflict, the Christian community is called to stand in the midst – the in-between space – identifying with the hopes and aspirations of the poor and oppressed for liberation and justice, but also as a minister of reconciliation. The cross, which Jesus chose, was the decisive historical and redemptive act. It is the only possible Christian response. Taking up the cross often exposes the Christian community to attacks from both sides of the conflict. Standing in the midst of conflict, however, breaks the cycle of oppression/retaliation with the creative action of loving the enemy.

Those who repay evil with good take the initiative away from the enemy. Love of enemy is a creative action that interrupts the cycle of evil justifying evil. It is that 'perfect love which casts out fear' of the enemy. It is not a soft option, even less is it a pious response. Neither is it submission to the enemy. Rather it is a creative and courageous act which has the power to make an ally of the enemy. It is fear that inspires the question, 'How can I protect myself against the enemy?' Love of enemy recognises that he (or she) is my responsibility, and that I have a duty and a creative opportunity to free him from his hostility. Evil is not overcome by extinguishing the enemy but by liberating him into a situation where our mutual freedom ensures our mutual survival.

It is a far better objective than 'change or disappear'.

✎ ✎ ✎

We have said that the kingdom is like light in a dark and colourless world, exposing what is evil and illuminating the signs of good that may be there. Christian mission in contemporary society must reflect this illumination. We have said that the kingdom is like salt in an unsavoury and savourless society, destroying what is rotten and adding flavour to that which is bland and without meaning and purpose. Christian mission in contemporary society must reflect this cleansing and seasoning. The kingdom is also like a little bit of yeast hidden in a lump of dough. How it fills the entire mixture, unseen yet potent! Every part experiences its power and influence. It is the power and influence of servanthood. The Christian community's mission must be permeated with this servanthood.

✎ For Reflection/Discussion

Mission is taking on the evil structures of our world and *doing* something concrete about injustice. We are called to 'stand' and 'resist' these structures.

In this chapter I have suggested some ways in which the Christian community may start to engage the structures – standing with the oppressed, and resisting those who oppress them.

Solidarity. We face common global problems, problems without borders. We have as much to learn from the poor as we have to share with them. Relationships and partnerships across the divides of wealth, race, culture can create understanding and reconciliation, and can begin to restructure human relationships and partnerships in such a way as to make justice and peace a possibility.

Advocacy. When we are in relationship and partnership with the poor, we may become their voice where theirs has been silenced by oppression and violence. Martin Luther King, Mother Theresa of Calcutta and Archbishop Desmond Tutu would be some examples of people who have done this.

Direct action. One of the best recent examples of this is the church in South Africa. Direct action in their case meant prayer beamed directly at the root of the injustice. It meant protest, imprisonment, suffering, grieving, organising a community to use whatever power it could amass *peacefully* against the injustice; this led to further suffering. Many times it meant standing in the middle of conflict as ministers of reconciliation. It always meant using weapons of warfare that were *spiritual* and *moral* rather than military and carnal. And it always meant operating from a position of extreme vulnerability and weakness. God defeated the powers by dying on a cross!

Changing sides. This means taking the side of the poor and looking at reality through their eyes. I have often been told by Christians in the West that the daily news is depressing or violent, and that they would not like to expose either themselves or their children to the daily litany of global suffering. I have always found this to be a worrying approach. When I watch the news, I could be watching the story of my own relatives and their suffering as I too come from a background of poverty and oppression. When I watch the news it is not simply global horror, but the story of some human being's mother, brother, sister, father, husband, wife, daughter or son. They wouldn't want the story of their lives to be avoided or trivialised as a bit of celluloid that could be turned on or off.

1 What relationship or partnership does your church community have with the poor (any community of poor and oppressed people)? In what ways are you advocates for those who are voiceless?

2 As a discipline, try to watch the news of global events from the perspective of the suffering and of the victim.

❧ *Notes*

1 J D Douglas (ed), *Let The Earth Hear His Voice*, Minneapolis, Minn (US): Worldwide Publications, p40.

2 Extract from *The Manila Manifesto: Final communiqué of the Lausanne II Congress on Worldwide Evangelisation*, Manila, 1989, pp4–5.

3 F Kefa Sempangi, extract from an article that appeared in *Eternity* magazine, December 1978.

4 Daniel Berrigan SJ, *Consequences, Truth and . . .*, The Macmillan Company, 1971, back cover.

5 John Stott, *Issues Facing Christians Today*, Marshall Pickering, an imprint of HarperCollins Publishers Ltd, © 1984, p136.

6 Morris Stuart, 'A Black Odyssey', unpublished manuscript.

7 Ronald Sider, *Christ and Violence*, Lion Publishing, 1980, p66.

❀ Chapter 7 ❀

Responsible Ecology – Caring for Creation

The physical creation has taken a battering at the hands of human beings. We are choking on the fumes of our affluent lifestyle. Yearly we reduce the stock of creatures in the global ecology, culling elephants into extinction for their tusks and depleting the ozone layer by excessive greenhouse gas emissions. We are spilling oil and using chemicals to clean up the mess. In the quest for economic development we are destroying the cultures of First Nations and aboriginal peoples and hence the valuable wisdom of those who have learned to *live with* the environment rather than leech off it.

Yet we are still disputing whether our planet is on a certain course to ecological disaster. Two recent publications by British academics, *Small is Stupid* and *Living on a Modern Planet*, have challenged the environmental orthodoxy. These publications actually propose that too much ecological 'responsibility' could wreck the international economy. They assure us that we could have much more industrial development and feed much larger populations. They attempt to set up a new orthodoxy, a coherent set of economic 'ethics' to bolster and sustain modern society's love affair with rampant and inexorable affluence. This wouldn't be the first time that intelligent people have reinterpreted the evidence before their very eyes in pursuit of short-term agendas for human gratification. They will have to be challenged with rigorous intellectual argument, with an alternative vision of the creation and with action to defend and care for it.

Creation is the divine project. Conceived in the imagination of God, every blade of grass, each colour of every flower, every microscopic human cell and every crimson sunset expresses the divine will and character. God does not engage in non-essential activity. We can assume that God attaches a great deal of significance to all creative activity, because each part and the entire whole is an eloquent statement of the divine nature and character.

The heavens are telling the glory of God;
    and the sky proclaims work of God's hands.
Each day praises it, each night heralds it

– without words or speech! –
to the very extremities of creation.

In this wonder of creativity, the sun ever emerges
[with joy] like a bridegroom leaving the bridal chamber,
    [with purpose] like a strong man it runs its daily course,
pouring its warmth into every nook and cranny of creation.
                                        (*Psalm 19:1–6, adapted*)

Too often Christians have treated creation like a sideshow,
a prelude to the main event which is the human creature.
As a result they have failed to see the creation as significant.
Yet even a cursory reading of the scriptures reveals a God
engaged in the work of creation with care and with purpose:
'In the beginning God created the heavens and the earth'.

At every stage of the creation story, the divine care and
delight shine through. From the creation of light and sky to
dry land and vegetation, from the creation of day and night
to sun, moon and stars, from the creation of bird, reptile and
animal life to the human creature, there is the unmistakable
stamp of divine attention to each detail. From naming to
feeding, from purpose through procreation, God treats the
creation project with seriousness. And at the conclusion of
each creative phase God pronounces the divine seal of
approval: 'God saw that it was good'.

Clearly the creation project was not an insignificant component of the kingdom enterprise. It was as important as
any other aspect of God's work. Delicately God balanced
the galaxies with their moons. With infinite care he placed the
sun so that its radiation would be nurturing not destructive.
On the earth the ecosystems were arranged in a relationship
of delicate interdependency, so that across the entire green
planet all things would cohere, mutual dependency ensuring
mutual benefit, mutual care ensuring mutual survival.

That we face today an ecological crisis of massive and
possibly suicidal proportions is self-evident. The depletion
of the ozone layer, the inevitability of global warming, the
massive extent of sea and river pollution, the devastation
brought about by acid rain in the industrial northern hemi-
sphere, the ever-present problem of the disposal of the waste
of Western nations and the destruction of the tropical rain
forests all witness to this crisis. And there is the ever-present
reality of unrelenting urbanisation with its impact upon the
green planet. The creation is indeed groaning like a woman
in childbirth (Rom 8:22).

The rise of the conservation movements world-wide, and the fact that they are now regarded as major grass-roots political forces to be reckoned with, indicate that society has had to respond to this concern. The Christian community, because of its concentration upon the 'soul', has until recently largely opted out of this issue, which is a pity.

The creation narratives, some Old Testament psalms and the restoration passages in the New Testament all indicate the passionate divine concern for the creation. We could say that God is the original and most passionate 'greenie'. This biblical vision is no latter-day trendy position such as that adopted by desperate radicals casting about for another hook to hang the gospel on. It is a vision motivated not by self-interest or survival but by stewardship. God, the keeper of the creation, calls the Christian community to do the same:

And God blessed them, and God said to them, 'Be fruitful and multiply, and fill the earth and subdue it; and have dominion over the fish of the sea and over the birds of the air and over every living thing that moves upon the earth.' (*Genesis 1:28*)

Poachers, hunters, mining magnates, entrepreneurs and evangelists for capitalism have regarded this statement as giving human beings – especially themselves – the right to exploit the creation's resources with relentless vigour. But this creation blessing is not *carte blanche* to appropriate the creation's resources either for private gain or for personal profit. Rather it is an invitation to stewardship and trusteeship. And we do not have to debate the meaning of 'dominion' and 'subdue'. We simply have to ask ourselves, 'How does God have dominion over us, or subdue us?' The answer is to be found in the example of Jesus, the divine servant. God rules by serving not by exploiting. It should be clear, then, that raping the earth and exploiting its resources is *not* an expression of 'dominion' or of 'subduing', which principally represent an invitation to serve the Creator's creation.

It is not our intention in this chapter to examine any of the theories of creation or the biblical creation story. We will not discuss whether 'evolutionary science' is right or 'creation science' is wrong, or what variants of either contradict or complement each other. The creation enterprise is bigger than either of these 'sciences'. We will not even discuss whether the biblical creation is literal or historically accurate as to its detail. These are important matters but they are not directly related to our purpose.

We do regard the early chapters of Genesis as God's truth in inspired literature, and as such these chapters contain helpful and constructive motifs that throw enormous light on the questions of existence, evil, religion, God, human relationships and responsible ecological behaviour.

ভ ভ ভ

There are five major biblical perspectives that make it clear that the creation blessing is not an incitement to destroy but an invitation to subdue, not subjugate, to serve, not dominate, to live with the Creator's creation and not to leech off it.

1 Creation and the character of God. 'Ever since the creation of the world his invisible nature, namely, his eternal power and deity, has been clearly perceived in the things that have been made' (Rom 1:20). The creation is not here simply for the benefit of its human creatures. It has a broader purpose. God is Creator, and the creation bears testimony to the divine identity and character: 'The earth is the Lord's and the fullness thereof' (Ps 24:1). It is not simply that God is the owner of creation, but especially that creation is the treasury of the divine wisdom, the laboratory of the divine Spirit and the statement of the divine character. This is where God works. This work expresses the Creator's character. We expect to 'read' God in the creation.

This is why the psalmist says that 'the heavens are telling the glory of God'; why the skies proclaim the work of God's hands; why day and night, springtime and harvest, children and old men, frolicking lambs, the whale, the stars and the mountains all express the divine creativeness and speak of the divine character. God's character is expressed not only in the kaleidoscope of colour, form, season, texture and balance; it is also expressed by the divine care over creation:

'Look at the birds of the air: they neither sow nor reap nor gather into barns, and yet your heavenly Father feeds them . . . Consider the lilies of the field, how they grow; they neither toil nor spin; yet I tell you, even Solomon in all his glory was not arrayed like one of these.' (*Matthew 6:26,28–29*)

This is the meaning of dominion and subduing. The Creator creates and thus rules. Creation expresses and affirms the Creator's benevolent character in a kaleidoscope of praise.

Polluted streams, forests destroyed by acid rain, barren mountain-sides, disfigured landscapes and beaches littered with syringes and other human waste do not extol the glory of God. They testify to the greed and indifference of the human creature. They are the result of the twisting of the Creator's instructions to us to subdue the earth.

The Creator's call to care for the earth does not imply only one option, that of a static agricultural economy. In any case, the final vision of the kingdom is not a pastoral property but a celestial city. Implied in the creation mandate is the expectation of development, of husbandry, of human management of land and animals for food, and of human discovery. All this is possible within the option of caring trusteeship rather than aggressive exploitation. Caring trusteeship does not allow for overstocking of land, harvesting and stockpiling of unsaleable crops for any reason. Nor does it mean hoarding.

If the creation expresses the character of God, and if God calls upon human creatures to care for it, then the current ecological crisis presents the Christian community with an enormous challenge. The creation in crisis is telling lies about the character of God and about its stewards who are supposed to care for it! The perspective that the creation expresses the character of God provides a framework as well as a motivation for the Christian community to care for the green planet. Ecology is our business because it is a commitment to protect the creation dream.

2 Till the earth and keep it – a garden motif. The creation is a garden to be tended not a quarry to be mined: 'And the Lord God planted a garden in Eden . . . The Lord God took the man and put him in the garden of Eden to till it and keep it' (Gen 2:8,15).

God is a gardener and not a miner. Thus the image is placed in a garden 'to till it and keep it', to 'garden' it on behalf of the True Gardener. We do not own the garden but we are far more than just tenant farmers. In the creation dream we are the divinely appointed rulers over the creation, the garden. This appointment carries with it the freedom to develop the garden in co-operation with the Master Gardener. The motif of the creation as a garden is the most appropriate for expressing the will of a benevolent Creator concerning the creation for a number of reasons:

蛿 The garden motif teaches us a fundamental lesson. We are to *live with the creation* and not exploit it to destruction. Our survival depends on its survival. A garden will produce for its gardener if the gardener tends and cares for it; no tending or care, no produce! 'Till it and keep it', and it will keep you. If we feed the garden, it will feed us. Such mutual dependency is the principle in all creation. If we rule over the creation as responsible gardeners, then the creation will forever provide a home with sustenance for us. The garden motif also intensifies our awareness and appreciation of the work of God's hands, engendering a respect for this treasury of the divine wisdom. As a result this understanding acts as a disincentive to junking creation. A gardener has constantly to tend the garden. The more the gardener tends it, the more the garden reveals to him the wonder of creation. The more he sees this wonder, the more he respects the work of God.

The pygmy people of Africa, East-Asian hill people, South American bush tribes and Aboriginal Australians have always known this. Christians, who have within their hearts the Spirit of the God of this creation and who have considered those 'others' to be pagans, have so often been blinded by their greed against the vision of God the Gardener. They have created instead a God who is a miner and, taking their cue from this God of their imagination, they have proceeded to rape the earth, bolstered by a capitalist vision of rampant and unrestricted development.

The Australian writer, Jonathan King, has aptly described this attitude: 'If it moves, shoot it; if it doesn't, chop it down.' To which we might add, 'And if it's in the ground, dig it up.' A garden is ruled over and subdued by care and by service. This is the way in which human beings ought to relate to the creation.

 The motif of the garden celebrates *the delicate balance between human responsibility and divine generosity*. Unlike the unrelenting predictability of the modern industrial process, gardening celebrates the effort and creativity of the gardener. It also exposes the gardener and the garden to the unpredictability of the flux and change of the natural elements. Agriculture is a risky business. If the creation is viewed as a garden, then there is an implication that the gardener will have to celebrate his or her craft in the context of God's grace and generosity. Gardening always implies faith and trust in the God of the elements. Environmental concern cannot be unhitched from divine sovereignty. Ecology cannot be unhitched from theology.

A garden is a renewable resource. As such it is a powerful picture of creation. A mine isn't! The cycle of seasons in the natural world testifies to this principle of renewal; so does the cycle of birth, life and regeneration. A garden is tended; it then gives produce. Its produce provides the seeds for regeneration which invites more tending. Such tending yields 'fruit' for the gardener's nourishment. Such is the perpetual cycle of gardening. This motif implies that the Creator's creation can be managed in such a way that perpetual renewal and perpetual sustenance are possible.

Many contemporary theories of development and economic management make a fundamental mistake: the wealth of nations and the development of economies are so often based not on renewable resources but on those natural resources that we already know are running out and for which there is no possible replacement. This is because we see the creation as a quarry and not as a garden.

Recognising that God views the creation as a garden does not imply that the ideal and only way for humans to respond to the creation mandate is to develop a primitive and static agricultural economy. There is no fixed law which states that ecological responsibility means things must be left alone in their raw natural state 'as God made them'. There is within the creation mandate room for development. This is implied in the invitation to the human creature 'to till the earth, subdue it, and have dominion over it'. The creation is a resource to care for, to tend and to live with. It is to be developed in co-operation with the Creator. It is to be worked in such a way that its renewable qualities are preserved. Agriculture, industrialisation, mining, technology and all other aspects of development can be pursued within a context that recognises the central and motivating vision of the creation as a garden. The garden motif allows for the aesthetic as well as the economic. It celebrates the delicate balance between beauty that refreshes and industry that replenishes.

3 Creation and sabbath. The creation is not there to be worked constantly, pursued relentlessly and exploited without respite. Here again the motif of the garden is instructive. The creation needs rest. The sabbath is not some unreasonable legalism imposed on human beings by a despotic deity; it is the provision of a benevolent Creator for our benefit. After the creation work was finished, God rested. The image of God is told to do the same. All creation needs rest and replenishment. This is its principle of renewability.

'Six years you shall sow your field, and six years you shall prune your vineyard, and gather in its fruits; but in the seventh year there shall be a sabbath of solemn rest for the land, a sabbath to the Lord; you shall not sow your field or prune your vineyard. What grows of itself in your harvest you shall not reap, and the grapes of your undressed vine you shall not gather; it shall be a year of solemn rest for the land.' (*Leviticus 25:3–5*)

This instruction, given to the ancient people of Israel, was for the benefit of the inhabitants of the land: 'Therefore you shall do my statutes, and keep my ordinances and perform them; so you will dwell in the land securely' (Lev 25:18). But the sabbath was also for the benefit of the land itself which had to have its rest if it were to maintain its productive purpose within the economy of Israel. This was a serious matter to the God of Israel. Failure by God's people to allow the land its rest could result in serious penalties for them:

'I will scatter you among the nations, and I will unsheathe the sword after you; and your land shall be a desolation, and your cities shall be a waste.

'Then the land shall enjoy its sabbaths as long as it lies desolate, while you are in your enemies' land; then the land shall rest, and enjoys its sabbaths.' (*Leviticus 26:33–34*)

This is the judgement for disobeying the idea of sabbath. God will save the land, even if it means sending the people into exile so that the fertility of the soil can be protected and ensured. The relentless exploitation of the soil leads to exile of the race. Modern ecologists are much closer to the biblical vision than many Christians when they assert that the earth will have its rest after the destruction of the human race. It is a warning that we ignore at our peril. Such avoidance only hastens the judgement.

Modern society has totally ignored the principle of sabbath. In the United States, Europe and Australia relentless farming and the continuous use of chemical fertilisers have resulted in the poisoning of the soil and lower than acceptable levels of agricultural production. As a consequence the soil now has to be chemically force-fed in order to produce the goods. Excessive clearing of the wooded landscape, especially in Australia and in the southern Philippines, has led to serious salt problems in the soil, rendering it barren and almost useless. In South America and Asia the clearing of rain forests and their alienation into grazing and agricultural estates have produced short-term benefits (less than five years in many cases), but have resulted in permanent ecological damage in the form of massive soil erosion.

The over-fishing of the seas and the oceans, the continuous exploitation of some natural resources, the expulsion of pollutants into the atmosphere and into the waterways and the consequent overburdening of the environment with waste all indicate our pressure on this fragile planet. The refusal to observe the principle of sabbath means that the environment has not been allowed its pause to breathe and to replenish itself. It will continue to break down until its human destroyers are themselves destroyed. Then it may have its sabbath, its rest. But this process can be halted if we accept and practise the idea of replenishing – the sabbath rest for all creation.

4 Creation and restoration. God's kingdom work includes the restoration of the cosmos to its rightful place, status and balance. In both the Old and New Testaments, passages that deal with the theme of restoration are peppered with idealistic ecological imagery:

The wolf shall dwell with the lamb,
    and the leopard shall lie down with the kid,
and the calf and the lion and the fatling together,
    and a little child shall lead them.
                                    (*Isaiah 11:6*)

The prophet Amos paints a picture of the environment not only at peace with itself but well-rested and eager for agricultural production:

'Behold, the days are coming,' said the Lord,
    'when the ploughman shall overtake the reaper
    and the treader of grapes him who sows the seed;
the mountains shall drip sweet wine,
    and all the hills shall flow with it.'
                                    (*Amos 9:13*)

As we have already indicated, in the New Testament the final vision of creation restored is not as a pastoral property but a celestial city. But even here the images are of a harmonious and generous ecology:

And I saw the holy city, new Jerusalem, coming down out of heaven from God . . . (*Revelation 21:1*)

Then he showed me the river of the water of life, bright as crystal, flowing from the throne of God and of the Lamb through the middle of the street of the city; also, on either side of the river, the tree of life with its twelve kinds of fruit, yielding its fruit each month; and the leaves of the tree were for the healing of the nations. (*Revelation 22:1–2*)

The physical creation is where the Creator and the Creator's image meet. It is the loving context of their mutual transactions. It continues to be the treasury of the divine wisdom and the laboratory of the divine Spirit. It is therefore never expendable in God's economy and is worthy of the same appropriate care that God lavishes on the image, the human creature. These three are bound together: the Creator, the Creator's image and the Creator's creation. They share a singular destiny, hence Paul's eloquent summary:

We know that the whole creation has been groaning in travail together until now; and not only the creation, but we ourselves, who have the first fruits of the Spirit, groan inwardly as we wait for adoption as sons, the redemption of our bodies. (*Romans 8:22–23*)

5 Creation and shalom. The Creator, the creation and the image belong together. When Adam and Eve sinned, their action had cosmic consequences. The creation came under a curse. Alienation replaced harmony. Drudgery replaced creative work. Subduing and ruling over was replaced by exploitation. Later, Israel broke her convenant. The consequence of this disobedience was ecological disaster:

... the land mourns,
    and all who dwell in it languish,
and also the beasts of the field,
    and the birds of the air;
    and even the fish of the sea are taken away.
                    (*Hosea 4:3*)

All creation is interconnected. There are cosmic consequences to human obedience and disobedience. In the beginning the consequence of human obedience was fellowship with God in the garden in the cool of the day. This was a picture of shalom, life in the creation as it was meant to be with nothing more to wish for.

ↂ ↂ ↂ

This is the creation dream, and in it is contained all the motivation for ecological concern and action based on a recognition that the creation expresses the character of God. This is the Creator who creates a garden and invites us to care for it and keep it, who gives the creation rest and the opportunity to replenish itself, who ever maintains the hope of a renewed and restored creation of shalom that reflects the creation dream.

There can be no doubt that the Christian community is called upon to exercise responsible ecology towards the physical creation. For theological as well as ecological reasons, this call cannot be relegated to a voluntary or optional interest of a few disciples. It is as much a priority within the kingdom enterprise as any other aspect of discipleship. Consider the impact on our society if the Christian community responded to this call faithfully and consistently.

Modern humanity would have saved itself the great ecological crisis if it had been more mindful of the creation, regarding it as a treasure to be cared for rather than a mine to be plundered.

🌸 For Reflection/Discussion

1 Consider two contrasting attitudes:

Creation in ecological crisis is lying about the character of God. Too often Christians have regarded the physical creation as expendable, a sort of sideshow. Consequently, they may come to judge conservationists to be creation-worshippers and pantheists.

Creation bears testimony to the character of God. God's work in the physical creation is important in revealing his overall purposes (see Gen 1; Rom 8:18–25). Taking account of creation must form a vital part of Christian worship and praise, teaching on the Christian faith, and Christian discipleship, so that we come to understand the self-disclosure of God (see Rom 1:18–21).

2 In 1994 the United Nations held an international conference on population in Cairo. The focus of the conference was on developing a global population policy designed to limit, stabilise and eventually reduce the world's population, as a necessary step to tackling pressing problems of global need. How does this relate to the statement in Genesis to 'multiply and fill the earth'? What are the challenges of this contrast for worship, teaching, faith and the action of the church?

The Human Creature – the Divine Image

For centuries philosophers and prophets, poets and visionaries have encouraged our hope for sanity in a world gone mad, for kindness and justice in a cruel world. Michelangelo and Plato, St Francis of Assisi and Martin Luther King, Bob Dylan and John Lennon have all inspired us and pleaded with us to create, to love, to overcome, to hope and to 'imagine'.

Few would dispute that in spite of all the beautiful things which humans enjoy on this planet, our world can be a pretty sick place. There is a problem when one-fifth of the world's people use four-fifths of its resources and are still not satisfied with their lot; when four-fifths of the world's people are inadequately housed, fed and educated, while the other one-fifth not only hoard their resources but steal from the future by plundering the earth's resources without regard for the needs of their children and their children's children.

We have a problem when, in the name of progress or, perhaps more accurately, greed, human beings mount an unrelenting assault on this fragile green planet, attacking the very things that are essential for our survival: air, water, the soil and the diversity of bio-organisms.

We are in considerable trouble when the most educated society is arguably the most psychologically traumatised. Today we know more about the universe and the physical world than ever before. Communication technology and the information revolution have made us the most informed society since the beginning of the human race. We know more about the human psyche than ever before, but we are still searching for ourselves. Possessing everything, we have nothing. We have gained the world, but are left wondering whether we have a soul.

There is no doubt that our world needs salvation, however understood, and justice, however defined. The key player in this dilemma is the human creature, the one without whose salvation and justice, there is no hope for a creation that is 'groaning like a woman in childbirth'. So, what is the human being? How valuable is he or she? Are humans the creatures of fate in a world of chance, pieces of cosmic dust in a harsh galactic desert? Is human life a lottery, a planned economy or a victim of circumstance?

We have explored why responsible ecology is an essential component of the kingdom enterprise. Now we need to see that the human creature's salvation and justice are equally important components. The creation project is significant. It is also vast in scope. Its size almost defies measurement. The vastness of the creation, its contemporary ecological crisis and the failure of the human creature to fulfil the original mandate to care for it present us with a number of problems.

First, the human being's place within the current ecological debate is that of the destroyer, the 'criminal'. Such a judgement may well be a justified one. Also, within the context of scientific discussion, the human being is often reduced to the status of a small bio-organism on a remote green planet and therefore insignificant within the universe's scheme of things. Modern astronomy and astrophysics indicate that the physical universe is apparently limitless in expanse. Often the effect of this is to 'cut the human being down to size'.

The question of the worth, status and value of the human being is an ever-recurring one. The Old Testament psalmist poses the dilemma in this way:

When I look at your heavens, the work of your fingers,
    the moon and the stars that you have established;
what are human beings that you are mindful of them,
    mortals that you care for them?

The answer packs quite a surprise:

Yet you have made them a little less than God,
    and crowned them with glory and honour.
You have given them dominion over the works of your hands;
    you have put all things under their feet...

                                                    (*Psalm 8, NRSV*)

These four lines of poetry propose a description of the human creature that is both audacious and breathtaking. No scientific formula, or philosophical statement, or conclusion of sociology or anthropology matches the simplicity and the wisdom of this statement from the Old Testament Book of Psalms.

Biblical literature abounds with images and descriptions of the unique and incomparable worth and value of the human creature who is described as being 'in the image of God', 'sharing the divine nature', more valuable than the rest of creation, of such worth and value that even in its most morally bankrupt state it is worth the most supreme divine sacrifice: 'God shows his love for us in that while we were yet sinners Christ died for us' (Rom 5:8).

In spite of the expansiveness (and magnitude) of the universe, and the physical minuteness of the human creation in comparison, its place within the divine scheme of things is significant and second only to the Creator in importance. We are made only a little lower than God who has appointed us to rule over the creation.

❧ ❧ ❧

How we view and value the human creature will determine how we treat a person. The scientific enterprise has invested a great deal of energy and intelligence to the benefit of humanity because of its presumed worth. Medical science expends a lot of effort and spends large sums of money on heart transplant and micro-surgery, not simply for the sake of scientific self-advancement but especially because the human creature is valued so much. Yet this same enterprise has at times appeared to regard prenatal and geriatric humans as expendable. Millions of dollars are spent on drug therapies and surgery to keep people alive (often artificially), yet modern science has given us the capacity to manufacture and deploy chemical and biological weapons whose use or very existence implies that human beings are expendable and it matters little in what manner they are extinguished.

It is an irony that the scientific enterprise praises as well as damns the human creature, celebrating both its worth and its worthlessness. What is responsible for this contradiction? The answer may be found in the scientific enterprise's starting point, by which the human creature is defined as a sophisticated machine, a most amazing coalescence of genes and chromosomes. All of this creature's actions, responses and even emotions, it is implied, may be scientifically understood and measured.

In the scientific enterprise, matters of origin, morality, spirituality and destiny are regarded simply as interesting, occupying the narrow gap between what science already knows about humanity and its world, and what science is still striving to know. As this gap narrows to extinction, so everything will be scientifically understood, measured and explained in mechanistic terms, which are the only terms by which we may understand the human creature anyway.

114

Aldous Huxley's *Brave New World* indicated to us a long time ago what a society that defined human beings scientifically would be like. It would be a dictatorship of the élite, a place where quality control was the rule of law, where only perfect specimens – members of a super-race – were valued and where others were specially bred to perform specialised tasks. In such a society all humans become slaves and prisoners of science and 'progress'. It is not a society that values the human creature for its own sake but only as a productive unit, a crafted, honed and tested specimen. Such a society has no place for Blacks, Indians, Aborigines, Down's Syndrome children, the physically or intellectually disabled and the mentally ill, as individual human beings.

This may seem to be an alarmist view. Yet if we removed questions of morality and spirituality from our deliberations concerning the worth and value of the human creature, we would be left simply with an amazing but fragile organism comprising 80 per cent water, worth – when melted down – a little more than a few dollars. Such an organism can only be valued in relation to its presumed usefulness to those who hold the power at a given time to dispose of or to preserve human life. George Orwell's *Nineteen Eighty-four* also clearly pointed out the dangers of using humans as tools for social engineering. No, the human creature is valuable, irrespective of race, age, natal status, sanity, criminality, stupidity, heredity or disability. It is a creature in the image of God and as such is of inestimable worth and value. No one has the right to tamper with this receptacle of the divine image. No one may oppress is, possess it, enslave it, ill-treat it, rape it, murder it or assume power over it.

❧ ❧ ❧

Human beings are not simply a little higher than the higher anthropoids, but a little lower than God (Ps 8). And the distance between the two measures is gigantic. However much we may share biologically with the anthropoids, our distance from them can be measured only in light-years. Conversely, our affinity with God is fundamentally close. No other creature is closer. We are 'in God's image', after the likeness but a little lower than God and potentially sharing his nature.

Starting points are important. This fundamentally close affinity is the basis for salvation and justice for the human creature.

Almighty God is creator ... In his mind the entire plan of creation was formed with man as the climax. Over the millions of years of geological history, the earth is prepared for man's dwelling or, as it has been put by others, the cosmos was pregnant with man. The vast forests grew and decayed for his coal, that coal might appear a natural product and not an artificial insertion in nature. The millions of sea-life were born and perished for his oil. The surface of the earth was weathered for his forests and valleys. From time to time the great creative acts ... took place. The complexity of animal forms increased. Finally, when every river had cut its intended course, when every mountain was in its intended place ... when every animal was on the earth according to the blue-print, then he whom all creation anticipated is made, man, in whom alone is the breath of God.[1]

In this eloquent statement Bernard Ramm focuses our attention upon the human creature as the centre-point of God's creation strategy. It is a reflection of the biblical record with its non-scientific assessments, which is unprejudiced and entirely equitable concerning the central place of all human beings in the divine scheme of things.

To be made in the image of God is to share that fundamental quality of existence. God is spirit, the essence of mind, phenomenal imagination and personality. As God is spirit, so the human creature has been created spiritual. We too are mind, imagination and personality. We are like our Creator for we are the very storehouse of God's breath.

When the human creature was created, we are told that God 'breathed into his nostrils the breath of life; and man became a living being'. In other words, it was this 'transfusion' of the divine breath of life that made the human creature a living being. This creative action was distinct from God's creation of other forms of conscious life; this 'breathing' points not simply to the creation of physical life, but especially to the quality and the kind of life that the human creature possesses. It is a life that comes from the very breath of God.

Further, by 'mind' we do not simply mean intellect, but moral intelligence. By 'imagination' we do not mean the ability to day-dream, but especially the capacity for creativity. By 'personality' we do not simply mean that which describes the quality or type of character, but the very definition of a kind of existence. God is personality: self-conscious, self-determined, moral and *ubiquitous*. The human creature is personality: self-conscious and self-determined but finite.

This is why God is the original and human beings are the copy, the image.

So our affinity to God is not physical but spiritual – moral, creative, intelligent, imaginative, personal and free. If this creature is shackled in any way, it is not simply an unfortunate violation of human rights, it is a blasphemous affront to the God in whose image it is made. Any oppression, possession, discrimination or tyranny against the human creature is an act of moral desecration. It represents a challenge to the Creator's work and a contradiction of the Creator's claim that we are made 'in God's image'. Furthermore, it harms both the perpetrator and the victim. Oppression is the 'big lie' about the human being. It tells us that oppressed human beings are worthless (dung!) and that those human beings who oppress others are nothing more than dung with power! This lie is an offence to God, and it has to be equally offensive to the people of God. Rooting it out is as important a kingdom work as any other.

The institution of slavery, the class war, the dictatorship of the proletariat, a society that is free to be unequal, racial segregation, global starvation, the few rich and the many poor, Apartheid, the Ethiopian/Eritrean war, the Gulag Archipelago are all realities that speak of man's inhumanity to man. They are all euphemistic descriptions of a singular tragedy – the sinfulness of human beings. How can this not be regarded as a fundamental concern of the people of God? Justice is the Creator's means of ensuring that the human creature is treated and behaves appropriately, as befits a creature who is made 'in the image of God'.

❦ ❦ ❦

To be made 'in the image of God' is to be made male and female: 'God created humankind in his image, in the image of God he created them; male and female he created them' (Gen 1:27, NRSV). We have already shown that God is spirit, one who is beyond gender as we understand it. Yet, as the 'original' the Creator possessed the qualities of female and male before human creation. God is the 'original'; we are the 'copy'. The biblical record consistently affirms the gender diversity of God. God is not only father but also mother, not only husband but also wife, not only captain of an army but also a hen who gathers her chicks under her wings.

Femaleness and maleness are essential to the image of

God. This implies equality of value and status between the sexes. In God's original creation, male and female are equal. There is no hint of hierarchy or subordination. The original creation mandate to subdue and to work the earth, to rule over creation and to procreate reinforces the notion of equality and makes it quite clear that either sex is indispensable to the divine image:

Then God said, 'Let us make humankind in our image, according to our likeness; and let them have dominion over the fish of the sea, and over the birds of the air, and over the cattle, and over all the wild animals of the earth, and over every creeping thing that creeps upon the earth.' ... God blessed them, and God said to them, 'Be fruitful and multiply, and fill the earth and subdue it; and have dominion over the fish of the sea and over the birds of the air and over every living thing that moves upon the earth. (*Gen 1:26,28, NRSV*)

There is no hint here of division of tasks or assignment of authority based on gender. The mandate to procreate and to rule is addressed to both the female and the male. Each has a gender that is different but both share a sexuality that is complementary. Their contrasting reproductive capacities and functions together fulfil the mandate to 'be fruitful and multiply and fill the earth'.

As separate and self-contained genders, the human creature represents an incomplete picture of humanity. Together, as two halves of the human race, they complete the picture of what it means to be made in the image of God. Paul's eloquent summary reinforces this unity: 'There is neither Jew nor Greek, there is neither slave nor free, there is neither male nor female; for you are all one in Christ Jesus' (Gal 3:28).

In God's original and good creation, male and female are equal and one. There was no hint of hierarchy or subordination of the female to the male. Neither was there any hint of division of tasks or assignment based on gender. They were different, but it was a difference reflecting a division of two from one. The human race has two branches but one tree, two genders cut from one essence.

In God's original and good creation, the woman is neither a doormat nor an employee, but a helpmate: equal, appropriate and in every sense a full partner with the man. Not out of his head was she taken so that she may rule over him; nor out of his feet was she taken so that he may rule over her. Woman was taken out of his side so that they may both be equal and bound together as evidence of the good image of God.

Hierarchy, sexual domination, divisions of labour, realms of responsibility and spheres of authority based on gender were never part of God's original and good creation but are the result of the Fall and the curse that ensued. Consequent upon the Fall, we are not presented with a new set of guidelines for governing human relationships. Repression, reaction and competition are all consequences of the Fall and its curse, and are not components of a new code designed to regulate human relationship for all time thereafter. The persistence of the image of God in the human creature (in spite of the Fall) and the work of Christ consistently challenge and work against the effects of the curse.

We have already established how illogical and contradictory it is for image to oppress image. It is equally illogical and contradictory to our survival as a race for gender to oppress gender. Like all other oppressions, it is an act of moral desecration against God's work and part of the 'big lie'. It is a frontal attack on the image of God and immediately and ultimately self-destructive. Either we celebrate our mutual image together, or we destroy that image together. There is no third way!

∽ ∽ ∽

To be 'in the image of God' is to be one species. The human creature comes from one stock – the 'image of God' stock. We belong to one race – the human race: 'And he made from one every nation of men to live on all the face of the earth . . .' (Acts 17:26). The new heavens and the earth will be populated by every tribe, tongue, people and nation.

Today we separate people into superficial, and at times artificial, 'racial' categories, all emphasising and accentuating our presumed differences: 'black', 'brown', 'white', 'red', 'coloured', 'civilised', 'uncivilised', 'primitive' and 'advanced'. The biblical record uses other categories: 'nation', 'culture', 'religion', 'clan' and 'people'. The differences among humans are not critical, fundamental and biological, but cultural. Physical characteristics are simply a fact of life and not really all that important. They are, in fact, part of the kaleidoscopic mosaic that is God's beautiful human creation and are never static.

The conventional wisdom today asserts that there are

fundamental differences which supposedly separate us from each other. The simple fact is we have more in common with our fellow image-bearers than we supposedly do not. This preoccupation with differences is simply another result of the Fall. Racial injustice and tensions all flow from this common source. They have been generated by the actions and attitude of people and societies. Racism expressed itself most effectively and disastrously through the structures of society, affecting its entire fabric. Apartheid in South Africa, continuing injustice towards black, brown and red people in the United States of America, the denial of justice to the original people of Canada, Australia and New Zealand and parts of South America are all expressions of sinful structural racism. The biblical record calls the people of God to resist such structures. First, we need to recognise, to accept and to celebrate our common image. Second, we need equally to recognise, to accept and to celebrate that God is bringing a new humanity into being.

Reconciliation is the lifestyle of that new humanity; the church – the people of God – is called to show it. Reconciliation is not the same as 'integration', that usually means making a racial minority conform to the cultural expectations of the dominant racial group. It is God who is at work in Christ, reconciling the world to himself, and who commits to the Christian community the work of reconciliation. We are to turn our belief in reconciliation into daily political, social and economic reconciling. The earliest Christian communities took this seriously. The leadership of the congregation at Antioch, for example, comprised Africans, Jews and at least one aristocrat, reflecting its multi-racial, multicultural and multi-class composition.

It was in the midst of a context of major social, racial and religious divisions that Paul called upon his fellow Christian disciples to build such communities of reconciliation which would truly reflect the restored image of God.

There is neither Jew nor Greek, there is neither slave nor free, there is neither male nor female; for you are all one in Christ Jesus. (*Galatians 3:28*)

 و ى ى ى

To be made in God's image is to be made creative. The human creature has been endowed with an instinctive creative capacity. We have a capacity to create after the

Creator – in poetry, art, music, writing, in forming and fashioning raw material with our hands. All humans have this capacity, irrespective of their status. All truth is God's truth. All beauty is God's beauty, and all of God's human creatures have a capacity to discover, to explore and to express this.

～ ～ ～

It is clear today that the human creature represents a contradiction of goodness as well as evil, of beauty as well as ugliness, of creativity as well as destructiveness. Obviously there has been some interruption to the good image of God. We have already discussed the Fall, how it radically altered the original creation context, how it had a detrimental effect on the original creation mandate, and how it marred the original image of God.

Humanity is in deep trouble, historically, socially, politically and personally. It is a situation that requires the most radical remedial action. But the Fall has fundamentally affected both humanity's ability to recognise its plight and its capacity to remedy it. Salvation is the divine answer. The Creator, who acted in the beginning to bring the image into being, now acts to restore that image and to reconcile the human creature. It is a testimony to the worth and value of man that God's love for us should be expressed in this way in that while we were so utterly morally bankrupt, Christ would die for us – the Godly for the ungodly, pure divinity for corrupt and sinful humanity.

Salvation is God's rescue plan for sinful humanity in deep trouble. It is also much more: it is God's affirmation of the fundamental worth and value of the human creature. It is precisely because of this worth and value that salvation and justice are necessary and indispensable to the kingdom enterprise.

🌾 For Reflection/Discussion

1 Discuss the following statements. Do you strongly agree or disagree with them?

There is a greater distance between human beings and the higher anthropoids than there is between human beings and God. We could say that God is our nearest relative. (See Ps 8, Gen 1:26; 2:7.)

The human creature is a mixture of goodness as well as evil. The good image of God is still resident in humans. It is now marred but not removed. If it were removed, humans would cease to be humans.

The salvation work of Christ is not just a statement of God's judgement upon human sin. It is especially and in the first instance, the most profound affirmation by God of our incomparable worth and value. (See Rom 5:6–9.)

Because God places such a high premium on the value of human beings, justice for them cannot be separated from their salvation.

2 In what ways does your church community link justice for human beings with their justification – in its worship, praise, teaching, fellowship and discipleship programmes? (See James 2:14–26.)

🎝 Notes

1 Bernard R Ramm, *The Christian View of Science and Scripture*, Paternoster Press, paperback edition, 1964, p155.

❧ Epilogue ❧

Letter from a Refugee

Dear (former) sisters and brothers,

I have handed in my Christian 'report card', so to speak. And I am lost! But I can't return to that 'Way' I once lived. It involved too much irrelevance, too much burying of my head in the sand, too much arrogance towards others. And I didn't even have a language with which I could address those 'lost souls', as we used to call them. If they are so lost, why do so many of them seem so much more together, more loving, caring, compassionate, just, zestful – in fact, so much more like Jesus – than I was when we were together?

Believe me, I tried. (I can almost hear you say, 'That was his trouble; he tried. He didn't rely on the Holy Spirit.' Wrong again! I was baptised 'in the spirit'. It was exciting stuff.) Yes, I did try. I read my Bible, eagerly, (almost) every day. I prayed and prayed and prayed. I sang and danced and marched and did my spiritual warfare. It was real. But it was a searching non-Christian friend who disturbed me with this question: 'If something is real, it isn't necessarily true, is it?'

That was my problem. I was searching all the time for the truth. In common with all the post-modernists out there in today's society, you were telling me that truth was experience. Over the years I found that in order to feel accepted in the church I had to separate my mind from my experiences, and separate both from the real world in which I lived and moved. When I asked questions, you cut me off with stories of your experiences. They were supposed to be total proof of God at work; and the more bizarre the experience, the more evidence this was of the presence and power of God. I knew God was mystery, but it seemed strange that God was so irrational. When the experiences were unconvincing to me, you capped it off by giving me half a dozen very powerful but totally irrelevant Bible quotations which, you said, would deal with my problem. But they didn't. In fact, as time went on, I found that I was beginning to hate the Bible. It used to be a light. You made it into a bludgeon. Sorry!

There were times when I was in such pain, but it was drowned out by the noise of the 'happy-clappy' songs. There was a limit to how many times I could sing the same three words. The more I sang them, the less effective they were. So I would crave new songs, and they kept coming, refreshing me for a while. As my 'refreshed' life collided with the pain of the wider world, however, I constantly found my experience inadequate to deal with the incredible needs, the injustices and the intellectual contradictions that confronted me daily. It seemed to me that the only contact we as a Christian community made with this world was to condemn it. Look, I'm probably overstating my case – the action of a very hurt person, I confess. But I am pouring out my mind and heart to you.

I got really embarrassed, sometimes very angry, when Christian spokespersons said things in the media. For the most part, they were ill-informed, irrelevant, arrogant and unintelligible. They just didn't seem to have a clue about the cultural currents out here in society. They didn't listen. They knew their language well and assumed that everybody else did. Such ignorance, and being so obviously out of touch, was tragic. And I remembered a Nazarene carpenter who told stories about the truth, and how the 'scum of the earth' gladly heard him.

This is why I was so elated and felt like worshipping God every time I heard about the suffering and courageous church in South Africa, because that church was at the forefront of the struggle for justice against Apartheid. I was amazed how Desmond Tutu could frame his prophetic words to the powers and the angry mob so effectively as he preached the gospel as we used to when I was with you. And when Mandela was freed and eventually justice triumphed, I went to a service of thanksgiving at an evangelical church community which had actually supported the ANC during the years of struggle. I sang songs of faith and freedom like I never did before or have since: 'Siyahamba Ekukhanyen 'kwenkhos', 'We are marching in the light of God'!

Yes, sisters and brothers in South Africa were marching to freedom, and the church was at the forefront of the struggle, suffering, bleeding, dying and, as grace would have it, being there to join in the victory procession as the powers were overcome, exposed and vanquished. That 'Praise the Lord!' was my most authentic; I still remember and cherish it. You rejoiced too. But I remember you criticising me for politicising the gospel when, many years before these events, I tried to share my concerns about Apartheid in our prayer group. Do you remember? You said to me, 'And what if they get their political freedom and are still dead in their sins?' Yes, I too had the same question upon my mind. But you seemed to me to trivialise their human suffering in that question. It was as if it didn't matter. I kept remembering Rodney. He was brutally beaten by the security forces and mysteriously 'killed' himself, falling out of a fourteenth-floor window at security headquarters in Cape Town. Rodney was a Christian. We prayed and studied the Word together. He was no communist or radical. He just believed in the justice of the kingdom for all South Africans. When you dismissed his sacrificial death in that question, it hurt; it really hurt. The tragedy is that you didn't even realise what you were doing!

So, my (former) brothers and sisters, what do I want? And what might have kept me amongst you? I say '*might have kept me*' because, knowing my human nature as I do, it may be that you could have done nothing to satisfy me. Some of us refugees are very demanding. I think sometimes I am a refugee by instinct. Nevertheless, if you could have had a restraining influence, the following things would have helped:

❦ It would have helped if I had had the freedom to ask my questions without my Christian integrity being questioned.

❦ It would have helped if our church community had taught me how to integrate mind and emotions.

❦ It would have helped if the outpouring of the Spirit had propelled us *en masse* to take the gospel of the kingdom to the poor, rather than use Spirit manifestation for our own self-indulgence. I found it hard to see in the scriptures that the 'refreshing' of God could be separated from the mission of God on the basis that this refreshing is for 'me' at the moment, a refreshing to deepen 'my' love for God.

❦ It would have helped if I had experienced, as a single person, the closeness of community. I had come to see that relationship was the highest structure in the universe because it was grounded in the character of God – Father, Son and Spirit. I really believed that we could have experienced something of this.

❦ It would have helped if our church was really immersed in our cultural context. No, not to copy every passing fashion;

but being there, being informed, understanding the symbols, the currents, the issues and the pain.

※ It would have helped if you had listened to the women and regarded them as equal in every sense. We would have been so much richer for their contribution.

※ It would have helped if our leadership was not so seduced by power and success, and instead really demonstrated servant leadership.

※ It would have helped if mission, in its broadest sense, was our passion: a kind of mission where our words were an explanation of our life rather than verbal assaults condemning people; where our deeds matched our words; where our worship was a celebration of justice rolling on like rivers, rather than morale-boosting sessions for so-called hard-pressed believers; where signs were in evidence but not as a spectacular show for its own sake; where our mission was illustrated by our life in community.

And when I was in my moment of deepest despair and knew that there was no God to comfort me, it would have been good if you had let me rave on and on, without trying to solve my problem for me; if you had just held me, saying nothing, soaking up my anger at God. Yes, it was my own fault that I left, but I wished I could have stayed. Sometimes it is lonely, perplexing and rough out here. But I have taken this step and, for the first time, I am savouring life as I want to. I have made some awful choices and am paying the price for them. Sometimes I think I hear 'the still small voice', but then I immediately remember the old days, and I shrivel up inside.

I sometimes remember the words, 'I believe in God, the Father, the Almighty, maker of heaven and earth . . . and in Jesus Christ his only Son . . . I believe in the Holy Spirit . . .' Once, in the cold light of day, with all the benefits of observation, information, reality, reflection and the gift of grace, I embraced them wholeheartedly. I really did believe that there was a loving Creator, Sustainer and Equaliser – Almighty God. I really did believe that in this God there was the key to those big questions of human origin, destiny, purpose and pain. Now I wonder. There are so many of us out here, and many others still among you who feel this way but just can't bring themselves to join us. And I wouldn't encourage them to either! For we have no answers, only lots and lots of questions, and, if there is a God there, we would like to encounter that God truly. I even feel that 'God' has not given up on us yet. I'll continue to search. I hope you will listen to me and search for a way to be authentic, so that I and the others out here could hear you and possibly, just possibly, re-join you.

In the meantime, although I am no longer your brother, because your Lord Jesus was a friend of sinners and outcasts I hope I can still remain your human friend,

Gregory Monkhouse, 'Refugee'